# Georgia Tales

## Stories of Georgia and Georgians

Ray Chandler

Pearl Mill Publishing 2017

Copyright © 2017 Ray Chandler
All rights reserved.
Pearl Mill Publishing

Cover: "Nancy Hart Confronts Tories" (Library of Congress)

ISBN: 1981335463
ISBN-13: 9781981335466

Library of Congress number: 2017958919

Second edition

All inquiries should be directed to Pearl Mill Publishing at
pearlmillpublishing@gmail

To the memory of my father, Raymond Edgar Chandler, to my mother, Sara R. Chandler, to my sister Rochelle M. Chandler, to the "Little Women," Shelby, Mary Beth and Brooke, and to Karen Seale in Yorkshire.

# Contents

| | | |
|---|---|---|
| vi | Foreword | |
| 1. | The Legend of Nancy Hart | 1 |
| 2. | "Ol" Dan Tucker was a fine ol' (real) man | 18 |
| 3. | The Tragedy of Beverly Allen | 26 |
| 4. | "Doc" Tommy Scott – Georgia's Merry Minstrel | 34 |
| 5. | Death Comes to "the meanest man in Georgia | 55 |
| 6. | Murder In Milledgeville: The Rage of Marion Stembridge | 68 |
| 7. | From A Georgia Chain Gang to the Great Escape | 90 |
| 8. | Up From Slave Row – The Making of William Henry Heard | 116 |
| | Notes | 133 |

# FOREWORD

At least since 1835, when Augustus Baldwin Longstreet published his *Georgia Scenes*, Georgians have loved tales about themselves. Longstreet's stories were fiction, though no doubt in part inspired by people he actually knew. These stories that follow here are all true. In the case of a couple, such as with Nancy Hart's story, as true as can be known. Some of the stories will carry readers far afield. They are about people who were born in Georgia or became Georgians and whose stories are part of the state's rich history. A few of the stories are about people – the Reverend William Henry Heard comes immediately to mind – that many might never have heard of, and it was time their stories were told.

One of my favorite quotes, for many reasons, comes from the British writer George Eliot (or, to use her given name, Mary Anne Evans):

"A human life, I think, should be well rooted in some spot of a native land, where it may get the love of tender kinship for the face of the earth, for the labors men go forth to, for the sounds and accents that haunt it, for whatever will give that early home a familiar unmistakable difference amidst the future widening of knowledge. The best introduction to astronomy is to think of the nightly heavens as a little lot of stars belonging to one's own homestead."

It should be the same, I think, with history as with Eliot's astronomy. There is no area of history that doesn't interest me. But none are more interesting than the history of Georgia and her people. Because it's our own, and some of the people involved are in our own bloodlines.

To understand ourselves and our place in the world, we must, like Eliot's wondering astronomer, understand our own history. That is why several of the stories included herein touch me personally. The people involved are kinsmen, near and far. My great-great grandfather, William Henry Mattox, whose acquaintance readers will make in these pages, was not a very good man by any standard, but he was very much a man of his time. He was an ambitious, striving man who prospered in the difficult years of Reconstruction by adapting to the changed postwar circumstances and applying his own ruthless nature. Mattox could have stepped out of any of several of William Faulkner's novels, but as some curious amalgam of a Sartoris and a Snopes. And he met a suitably Faulknerian end in a dusty road.

The Reverend William Henry Heard was a surprise to find. His rags to riches story of a sort I found while researching my 2015 book *The Last Days of the Confederacy in Northeast Georgia*. His story was one of two that was going to frame a chapter about the freed slaves of the northeast Georgia counties, but the chapter had to be cut in the final edit. Nevertheless, I wanted his story told. Going from a slave cabin on an Elbert County plantation to being the U.S. minister to Liberia (and along the way becoming a bishop in the African Methodist Episcopal Church) is an amazing story of an amazing man. And though I had absolutely no idea when I happened upon his story that he, too, would turn out to be a kinsman, he apparently was. That is a story in itself, and another brush stoke on the complex portrait of the history of the times in which Heard – and Mattox – lived.

Some of these stories have appeared in different forms under my name in magazines over about 25 years. Over time, though, different perspectives, new information, or just dissatisfaction with part of the result the first time has led me to rework former material to a way I do like it.

The lead piece, about Elbert County's own Nancy Hart, is a prime example. In 1999, I wrote a piece on the legend of Nancy Hart and her exploits during the American Revolution in north Georgia for what was then *North Georgia Journal* (later *Georgia Backroads*). It was the second story I ever wrote for the magazine and, frankly, I was a bit careless, too eager to again get into print. I relied too much on local lore without delving deeper into the subject. Following up on that, which included finding some entirely new materials overlooked before, completely changed my perspective and the whole story. Now, several score of magazine articles and several thousand newspaper articles later, I wanted to correct some errors.

The thing is, even though there is little doubt the stories of Nancy contain some kernel of truth that saw a lot – and I mean a LOT – of stretching, the stories lose little of their allure when subjected to our microscope. The stories may tell us little that we can rely on as history but they tell us a lot about the people who lived in the times in which the stories were first told, burnished, stretched beyond all recognition of the original article and finally grew into legend. I hope that some who might be peeved at seeing a good deal of the legend deflated find something to enjoy in the result.

Other stories, however, such as that from an interview with the late "Doc" Tommy Scott, Georgia's famous medicine show man, see print here for the first time. A fascinating man. He lived for his music and his audiences, and his story of his life and times was another filigree pattern in the story that's all of ours.

I hope any reader enjoys reading these stories at least half as much as I enjoyed discovering and writing them.

Ray Chandler
Elberton, Georgia
November, 2017
charlesrchandler@gmail.com

# 1

# The Legend of Nancy Hart

Nancy Hart, from 19th century print
(Library of Congress)

The place is about a mile north of the Broad River in upper Georgia, a few miles west of the Savannah River. The time could be spring, summer or fall – no one who told the stories of this day ever said what time of the year it all happened, but winter seems unlikely. A group of mounted men – various accounts will number them from three to six – splashed through the shallows of the lazy creek, urged their winded horses up the low bank and cantered toward a small, lone log cabin. Wispy blue smoke curled from the field rock chimney.

In short order their hails fetched the woman of the house. It's likely the smallest of her children cling to her tattered linen dress and peep around her at these strangers, in no small fear. The woman may herself also be afraid, but she was known for never showing it.

By all accounts, she was a woman who would have drawn the men's eyes but not their fancy. In the tales told of her she is described as being a shade over six feet tall and rawboned, with frowsy red hair and a pox-pitted face, "cross-eyed, with a broad angular mouth, ungainly in figure, rude in speech and awkward in manners … vulgar and illiterate, but hospitable and valorous." Not hospitable to these visitors, though.[1]

They were Tories, declared loyalists to the British Crown in the revolution being fought as a partisan war in the backcountry of the Carolinas and Georgia, and to the backcountry residents – often to loyalists and always to rebels – whether they were really fighting for their king or not they did a good business as scavengers. Her crossed eyes would have met them with a hard stare.

She was Nancy Hart, diehard rebel. And before the day was over her visitors would become unwilling players in the making of her legend. The story of her capturing these Tories and overseeing their hanging – true or not – will become one of the most told tales of this heroine of the American Revolution in upper Georgia.

Other stories passed down through time have her helping rebels on the run and foiling their Tory pursuers, dressing as a man to spy on the British in Augusta for local rebel leaders, leading the defense of a local fort against Indian attacks while the men are away. Another even has her taking part in the fighting against a small army of Carolina loyalists at the Battle of Kettle Creek in February 1779.

And all the while she was wife to her husband Benjamin, mother to at least ten children, an excellent cook (especially renowned for preparing pumpkin in myriad ways), a noted expert midwife and herbalist and, besides all that, as skilled a hunter as any man, often seen musket in hand stalking deer through the woods.

The stories about her have come to be regarded as true almost without question, even being cited in encyclopedia entries and quoted in histories with very little qualification. To others over the years and into the present, though, the stories seem too fanciful to be fact. In 1901, one ambitious but now scarcely remembered historian would even go so far as to claim that Nancy Hart never existed at all.

**Who was Nancy Hart?**

To begin with, that dilettante historian of 1901 was wrong. There was indeed a woman named Nancy Hart who lived in what is now Elbert County beginning in the early 1770s. She was born most probably in 1735 (some sources claim 1747) to Thomas and Rebecca Alexander Morgan, who lived originally in Bucks County, Pennsylvania. Like many in their area, Thomas and Rebecca Morgan followed trails south to the Yadkin Valley of North Carolina in search of new lands for the pioneering. It is uncertain, though, whether their daughter was born in Pennsylvania or after their move. It is also believed that she was named Ann at birth, with Nancy coming into use later as a familiar name among her family.[2]

Chroniclers of her legend have often over the years claimed her as a relative of both the legendary frontiersman Daniel Boone and General Daniel Morgan, the canny victor over the British forces at the 1781 Battle of Cowpens. The alleged connection to Boone comes through his mother, who was also a Morgan and also from the area of Pennsylvania from where Thomas and Rebecca Morgan hailed, as was Boone himself. (The Boones, incidentally, also migrated from that area of Pennsylvania to the Yadkin Valley before Boone began his treks into Kentucky.) In the early 1950s, however, the imminent Georgia historian E. Merton Coulter delved as deeply as possible, given existing records, into Nancy's lineage and found no documentary evidence of any connection between Nancy Hart and either Boone or Daniel Morgan.

Nevertheless, according to Coulter, Nancy Hart "was not a 'nobody'." She married Benjamin Hart, born in 1730 or thereabouts in Hanover County, Virginia, before ending up in the Yadkin Valley, and through Benjamin would eventually gain two famous relations. A daughter, Lucretia, of Benjamin's brother Thomas would marry Kentucky's native son and 19th century statesman Henry Clay after that branch of the Hart family settled in Kentucky. Clay, "The Great Compromiser," played a key role in shaping antebellum American politics and was the idol of Abraham Lincoln. Another niece would marry a North Carolina lawyer named Jesse Benton. That marriage would produce a son, Thomas Hart Benton, a celebrated United States senator from Missouri whose role in 19th century American politics would, like Clay's, make him a legend in his own right.

It's believed that by the late 1760s or very early 1770s the Harts, Benjamin and Nancy, had moved to what would later become the Edgefield District of South Carolina. By the mid-1770s, however, it is certain they had taken up residence in north Georgia, in what was a recent acquisition of land by the British government just opened to settlers.

In 1773, Georgia's royal governor, James Wright, arranged a deal by which the Cherokee and the Creek tribes would pay off a debt to merchants in Augusta, Savannah and Charleston by ceding to the British Crown a large area that now makes up much of northeast Georgia between the Little and Tugaloo Rivers. The land was opened to settlement, and in 1774 the Harts acquired 200 acres on Long Creek, not far from the Broad River that now forms Elbert County's southern, southwestern and western border and flows east-southeast into the Savannah River a few miles from where the Harts settled. Their neighbor owning the land just across the creek was Elijah Clarke, destined to gain fame as a rebel leader in the war to come.

What sort of people were the Harts one can only speculate. From the traditional description of Nancy, she seems to fit the general character of the backwoods folk of the Carolinas who were part of the settlers who filtered into the new lands opened in north Georgia. The Virginia aristocrat William Byrd traveled through the Yadkin Valley in the 1760s when the Harts lived there and observed that *"the men did little work. (They make) their wives rise early ... at the same time that they Lye and Snoer [sic] till the Sun has run one-third of its course."* A Moravian missionary echoed Byrd's sentiments, adding that farm work was neglected and livestock fended for itself as the men drank, hunted and fished.

Others were even less charitable. The Reverend Charles Woodmason, an Anglican missionary in the Carolina backcountry during the 1760s and early 1770s, described the backcountry folk he encountered as *"white savages ... ignorant, mean, worthless, beggarly ... the Scum of the Earth, the Refuse of Mankind."* The backcountry folk, Woodmason noted, provided themselves with only the very basics of food and shelter, had lots of children to whom they paid little attention, and their young girls (he noted particularly) were given to wearing the skimpiest of clothing and that deliberately drawn up tight-fitting. Couples frequently never bothered with formal marriages, owing to a scarcity of ministers, but often would later go through a ceremony if a traveling minister was available.

None of these commentators can be assumed free of bias. As a Tidewater aristocrat very well aware of his social class, Byrd would have hardly been inclined to look on the hardscrabble backcountry folk with favor. The Moravian missionary would naturally have found the apparent lax work ethic he observed appalling compared to his own traditionally industrious group. And Woodmason, who spent a good deal of his time in the upper crust society of Charleston, comes through in his journal as stiff and more than a little hidebound in his judgments, reflecting generally how the more cultured coastal residents saw the backcountry settlers, and thus apt to view the more libertine lifestyle of some of the backwoods folk with a jaundiced eye. The Anglican Church's traveling salesman faced an uphill battle anyway. A good many of those he wanted to bring into the fold were Presbyterians or Baptists, when they bothered with denominational religion at all, and were inclined to view the Anglican Church and all associated with as much suspicion as the backcountry folks received. Historian Grady McWhiney drew the most complete and nuanced portrait of these folk in his 1988 *Cracker Culture: Celtic Ways in the Old South*, but parts of his book still ring with those sentiments and observations of Byrd, Woodmason and others of like opinion.[3]

What all of these contemporary observers experienced, however, was a rudimentary society that had not yet taken firm root and sorted itself out, with the more dedicated and ambitious laying the foundation for a more stable and industrious community. Time would prove there were indeed a more industrious and far-looking number among the largely Scot-Irish and Welsh peasant stock and the down-at-heels Anglo-Irish, Scot and English gentry that settled the backcountry of the Carolinas and Georgia. Those bearing the later most respected names of the Georgia and South Carolina upcountry – such as Pickens, Calhoun, Heard and Clarke – all rose from this rough-and-tumble frontier. Bringing civilization to the wilderness took hardy folk, who often had little time for niceties. Benjamin Hart's rise over the course of his life marks him as one of these ambitious men, though less renowned.

He was, for instance, elected a captain in the local militia during the Revolution, a sure measure of the respect he commanded among his upcountry neighbors. After the Harts moved in 1791 from the Broad River valley to Brunswick on the coast, Benjamin again became a leading citizen there. In 1794, he was listed on the tax rolls as owning fifty acres in and near Brunswick and also as owning fifteen slaves, the second most slave owner in the county. (When the Harts moved to north Georgia in 1774, Benjamin owned seven slaves, which already set him apart from most settlers as a man of some means.) In 1796, he became a justice of the peace and later a justice of the local inferior court. He died in 1801.

Upon Benjamin's death, Nancy moved to what's now Clarke County, Georgia, to live with her second son, John, who owned a tract of land along the Oconee River. John, formerly the sheriff of Jackson County, had been appointed one of the commissioners responsible for establishing the new Clarke County and contracting to build its first public buildings. At some point – the exact year is not known – John moved his family, including his mother (who is believed to have been twice a widow by this time) to Henderson County, Kentucky. John died there in 1821, and Nancy is said to have continued to live there with his widow. If the date on her tombstone is taken as correct, Nancy herself died there in 1830.

**The legend grows ...**

In the 1870s, after the legends of Nancy Hart's exploits in the revolutionary backcountry had taken firm root, locals in the Athens-Clarke County area recounted family stories two or three generations old of relatives who had known Nancy and claimed to have heard her herself recount her exploits.

Earlier, in 1855, former Georgia governor George R. Gilmer, who had grown up in the Broad River area where the Harts had lived and who maintained that his mother knew Nancy Hart, recounted the stories about Nancy in his *Sketches of Some of the First Settlers of Upper Georgia, of the Cherokees and the Author*. Some of the biographical material Gilmer included, such as that after Benjamin's death Nancy moved to Alabama, is provably untrue but the stories are presented as stories told in the area where Gilmer grew up, passed down by people who had supposedly known the Harts. This may be true. But what can be traced of the birth and growth of legend of Nancy Hart leaves a lot of room for doubting the truth of the stories themselves as they are known, for the tales appear to have grown in the telling. Have grown in the telling, in fact, like kudzu.

When E. Merton Coulter took his own look at the Nancy Hart legend in the 1950s, he found it odd that the stories about Nancy did not appear in historian Hugh McCall's two-volume (1811 and 1816) *History of Georgia, Containing Brief Sketches of the Most Remarkable Events up to the Present Day*. If the stories of Nancy Hart were circulating out of the vicinity of Elbert, Wilkes and Oglethorpe counties, Coulter held, they would have been irresistible fodder for McCall, since this books dealt heavily with the heroes and deeds of the Revolution. What is true of McCall's book would also have been true for the 1822 book by a South Carolinian writer, Alexander Garden. Almost doubly true, in fact, for Garden's *Anecdotes of the Revolutionary War in America, with Sketches the Character of Persons Most Distinguished in the Southern States, for Civil and Military Purposes* (a book with, apparently, a very large cover and title page), for it contains a particular section "Conduct of the Whig Ladies." But Garden's book hasn't even a hint of Hart. It would not be long, though, before the stories met printer's ink.

The earliest mention in print of Nancy Hart that Coulter uncovered was in an 1825 edition of the Milledgeville *Southern Recorder*, with the story apparently picked up and reprinted in the Yorkville (S.C.) *Pioneer*. (More later about how Coulter established this.) The year of the first mention was a clue on which Coulter hung a great deal of completely plausible speculation. Why was 1825 a significant year for the Nancy Hart stories to make their print debut? Coulter speculated that the timing was related to the tour of the United States undertaken that year by the aged hero of the Revolution, Gilbert du Motier, better known to history as the Marquis de Lafayette. The Frenchman's tour of the young republic, regarded even by some at the time as a farewell tour (he would die in 1834), created excitement wherever he ventured. As Georgia's capital, Milledgeville was among his stops, and his visit was the occasion for a celebration. And there as everywhere else he went, his visit awoke a renewed interest in all happenings and people related to the revolutionary period.

It would have been natural, Coulter opined, for a newspaper writer who had somehow managed to hear any local oral traditions of Nancy Hart to publish the story without quibbling over possible embellishment (or perhaps even adding some himself for seasoning). This explanation on the timing of Nancy Hart first seeing print seems perfectly plausible, and is likely the way it happened.

The *Southern Recorder* and *Pioneer* stories (and perhaps other reprintings not documented) apparently attracted little attention because it was 1848 before Nancy Hart's stories again saw print. That year Elizabeth Fries Ellet published her two-volume *The Women of the American Revolution* and also an article in *Godey's Lady's Book and Magazine*, in both of which she recounted Nancy's wartime exploits. Ellet, a New Yorker, was the wife of a chemistry professor who had moved from Columbia College (now Columbia University) to a professorship at South Carolina College in that state's capital. In 1840, she had published her first book, *Rambles About The Country*, relating excursions through Virginia, the Carolinas and Georgia and including local lore picked up in her travels. Significantly, this book makes no mention of Nancy, the stories of whom would have been just the sort of item Ellet sought out. We seem on safe ground, then – Coulter thought so – to assume that before 1840 the local tales were still not circulating widely enough for Ellet to have heard them.

In 1849, George White, a minister also given to historical writing, published his *Statistics of the State of Georgia* in which he repeated Ellet's version of Nancy Hart's story, making some alterations but giving Ellet due credit. White also claimed that Nancy's famous relative Thomas Hart Benton, with whom White had corresponded, confirmed the stories. (Any knowledge Benton had of the stories would have been second- or third-hand at best.) In 1854, White published another volume, *Historical Collections of Georgia*, in which he again repeated Ellet's tale of Nancy but also included a sketch he credited to the Yorkville (S.C.) *Pioneer*. White did not give a publication year for the newspaper's sketch, but Coulter concluded that it was almost certainly a reprint of the *Southern Recorder* story because it was very similar to a version the dabbler historian Lucien Lamar Knight published in 1913 in the first volume of his *Georgia's Landmarks, Memorials and Legends* and attributed to an 1825 edition of the Milledgeville paper.

The tales themselves evolved over the course of their telling, a natural thing, being the only way little tales grow tall. The story told in the *Southern Recorder* and the *Pioneer* was a simple tale of six Tories showing up at the Hart cabin and demanding a meal, with Nancy providing one of roasted venison, hoecakes and honey. After the Tories foolishly stacked their muskets before attacking the meal, Nancy grabbed one, took the Tories prisoner and sent one of her children to fetch Benjamin and other local rebel men. The hapless Tories were then sent to their reward "according to the rules of the times."

By the time Ellet retold the story in 1848, five Tories from a raiding party out of Augusta who had just killed local militia leader Colonel John Dooly rode up to the cabin. They asked Nancy if the stories were true that she had recently helped a rebel being pursued by another group of their fellow Tories. Nancy owned to helping the rebel and told her visitors how she had done it. She had told the first Tories she had seen a rider turn off another path some distance from the cabin and the riders had gone off in pursuit. In fact, however, Nancy had had the rebel horseman ride through her cabin and out a backdoor as a way of obscuring his trail. Her seeming to boast of this ruse did not sit well with her new visitors and they demanded she give them food, one of them shooting a turkey in the yard and ordering Nancy to cook it.

They stacked their muskets in a corner of the cabin and applied themselves to a jug of whiskey while they waited for the meal. For her part, a sullen Nancy went about her cooking but took note of the stacked muskets. (In some later versions Nancy becomes convivial with her visitors, including taking her turn at the jug while bantering and joking, thereby throwing them off their guard.) She sent her daughter Sukey to fetch water from the spring and also to blow a conch shell (a conch shell in the north Georgia backwoods!) as an alarm to summon the menfolk. Meanwhile, she is passing the Tories' muskets outside through a space in the cabin chinking. (Why would she do that?) When one of the apparently deaf Tories notices this and springs to his feet, Nancy levels the musket in her hand on her visitors and orders them to surrender. Thinking the cross-eyed Nancy is not actually looking at him, one Tory tries to rush her. She shoots him dead and grabs up another loaded musket. She wounds another before her menfolk arrive, after which she oversees the hanging of the four left alive.

In Ellet's telling the very tree from which the Tories dangled was supposedly pointed out by a local resident in 1828. This was essentially the same story told by the Reverend White in his 1849 book. In 1851, George Gilmer, who would retell the Nancy Hart stories himself in his 1855 book, told an abbreviated version to an audience at Franklin College ( soon to become the University of Georgia) in which Nancy merely marched her prisoners to "Clarke's station," meaning, presumably, Elijah Clarke's nearby home.

By the time White published his second book in 1854, he had added six more stories. For two of these he credited a claimed relative of Nancy's then living in Baldwin County as the source. In the first, Nancy hurled boiling soap through a crack in her cabin wall into the eyes of a spying Tory. She then takes him prisoner. In the second, not at all related to the revolution, Nancy breaks her son-in-law out of the Burke County jail. The other four stories were, according to White, told him by a Mrs. Wyche of Elbert County, "a lady far advanced in years, who was on terms of intimacy with Mrs. Hart." (Mrs. Wyche, whoever she was, would have needed to be at least in her late eighties for this to be true.) These are the stories that have Nancy making a raft to cross the Savannah River to spy on Tories (no man would dare go, but Nancy did!), taking other Tory prisoners, leading the defense of a local fort full of women and children when a band of Tories and Indians attack while the menfolk are away, and finally, dressing as a man to sneak into Tory-held Augusta to spy for Elijah Clarke.

In his 1855 book, George Gilmer would add another story of Nancy taking on another local woman in a hair-pulling brawl. He does not give a specific source for the story other than to note it was simply a story commonly told. Stories of Nancy had become like some folk songs – everyone was free to add a verse of their own. But taken altogether, by the 1850s, the legend of Nancy Hart was firmly fixed.

So much so was the legend of Nancy Hart fixed as fact in the public mind by then that when the Georgia legislature went on a spree of county-creating in 1853-54, one of the thirteen new counties was named Hart County in her honor. (The creation of Hart County, carved out of Elbert and Franklin Counties, was pushed by two legislators from Elbert County, L.H.O Martin and E.L. Rucker.) The original intent was for the county seat to further honor her by being named Nancyville, but Hartwell it became instead.

Nancy also became the subject of a series of drawings and lithographs that found their way into wide distribution, and her legend continued to grow and spread throughout the state and likely beyond. When during the Civil War a group of women in LaGrange, clear across the state, organized themselves into a militia, they rallied to Nancy's memory, dubbing themselves "The Nancy Harts."

The writings of Ellet and White (with White citing the earlier 1825 stories) then are the root and branch of the Nancy Hart legend, for most other widely read historians and memoirists continued to ignore Nancy even while her legend grew. William Bacon Stevens, whom Coulter described as "the first historian of Georgia to use scholarly techniques in his researches and writing," did not mention Nancy in his 1859 volume, though by then the Ellet and White stories were common currency. Adiel Sherwood, like White a preacher-cum-historian, finally mentioned Nancy in the 1860 (and last) edition of his *Gazetteer of the State of Georgia* after not mentioning her in his 1827, 1829 and 1837 editions. Noting that Hart County was named for Nancy, Sherwood however added that "the stories told in fancy sketches ought to be taken with some grains of allowance." Noting that she was "said to have been a greater terror to the tories than a dozen men. … The accounts may have been exaggerated, but there is no question that she was an extraordinary woman, of great courage, Amazonian strength, and high temper."

Wilkes County's own Judge Garnett Andrews, in his 1870 memoir, *Reminiscences of an Old Georgia Lawyer*, doesn't mention the Hart stories at all, though his recollections went back as far as 1808 and his book is chockfull of arcane local stories that really aren't found anywhere else. Neither would Charles Colcock Jones, Jr. mention Nancy in his 1883 *History of Georgia*. That Andrews doesn't mention Nancy Hart as fact or legend is more telling than Jones's lacking, for Andrews grew up in the general area in which the Harts had lived, and himself lived and practiced law in Washington, Georgia, less than fifteen miles from Nancy's old stomping grounds. Nancy's legend was spreading, clearly, but not attracting all the notice you might expect.

It would take the better part of two decades and three other writers to complete the job of turning the legends of Nancy Hart into fact. The first, the best remembered, and the one whose retelling of the Hart legend probably carried the most weight was Joel Chandler Harris, celebrated newspaperman of the *Atlanta Constitution* and writer of, among other works, *The Uncle Remus Tales*. In 1896 he published his *Georgia Tales* and devoted a whole chapter to Nancy Hart, taking all the old tales at face value. "Neither fable nor invention," Harris wrote, "has touched the character or deeds of this heroine of the Revolution." (Ahem!)

Then in 1898 Lawton B. Evans published *A History of Georgia for Use in Schools*. Nancy Hart's stories would be taught as history to legions of Georgia schoolchildren. Finally, Lucien Lamar Knight, who would also write of Nancy in his 1913 book, noted in his *Reminisces of Famous Georgians* that "the story of her thrilling exploit is neither myth nor fable; and she bids eternal defiance to the higher critics." Harris's acceptance of the Hart stories as fact little doubt influenced both Evans and Knight to also cite them as such. Harris was a master storyteller well on his way to becoming a celebrated figure, but he was also a journalist of some eminence. He wasn't an historian, but it seems unlikely he was completely unaware of the provenance of the Hart stories, at least since their publication by Ellet and White. In that light his stamp of authenticity is all the more remarkable.

For those storytellers intent on making Nancy's exploits into historical facts beyond question, troublemakers continued to appear, though. In a 1901 interview with the *Atlanta Journal* the now forgotten historian George G. Smith claimed Nancy's exploits were "a story of fiction. There was no such person as Nancy Hart in real life. It is just a pretty story that was written by a clever writer, and it made such a hit that the character of Nancy Hart has been given a place in history." He attacked the 1825 *Southern Recorder* story as a total fabrication. It's not clear why Smith chose that instance to attack Nancy's legend but his timing was unfortunate. Because Nancy's defenders had the nerve to point out (gleefully, no doubt) that Smith had in his *The Story of Georgia and the Georgia People, 1732-1860*, published just the year before, cited Nancy as an historical character, "an intrepid Whig, who doubtless captured several Tories and had them safely hung."

Trapped on the flypaper of his own words, Smith acknowledged that Nancy had actually existed but still questioned the tales of her exploits as lacking foundation. No formal histories of Georgia had given credence to Nancy's adventures, after all, Smith maintained (ignoring that his own had), and Ellet and White, the apparent fountainheads of the tales others had repeated and built on, had not provided real evidence.

Despite Smith's contradictions, though, he had his defenders. One, J.M. Bosworth of Atlanta, took to the pages of the *Atlanta Journal* to offer his own reasons for doubting Nancy's oft told exploits. According to Bosworth, he had ventured to Elbert County in 1895 looking for artifacts related to Nancy to display at the Cotton States and International Exposition put on in Atlanta that year. Bosworth claimed to have interviewed several elderly people, including his wife's grandfather, and had come away empty handed. Some of the interviewees told Bosworth they had heard of Nancy Hart and her cabin, but his wife's grandfather told him he had never heard of either. A Dr. Turner, of Hartwell, told Bosworth that the tales of Nancy Hart were based on a woman named Nancy Rumsey, who had lived in the Goshen community of Elbert County. The Reverend George White, Turner said, had concocted the stories of Nancy Hart based on Nancy Rumsey. (Apparently it escaped the notice of both Bosworth and his cited good doctor that Ellet's account actually appeared first.)

Nancy's defenders leaped to the battlements with their own letters to the editor. Mrs. T.M. Green, regent of the Kettle Creek Chapter of the Daughters of the American Revolution, rushed to add that her father, born in 1798 and having grown up in the Harts' old community, had told her the stories of Nancy, though Green admitted that some of the tales "have of later years been somewhat exaggerated." Others of the Elbert, Wilkes and Oglethorpe County areas or with roots there added their own family oral traditions to show that the genesis of the tales – and thus proof of their authenticity – went back further than White, Ellet or the 1825 Milledgeville newspaper story. One Atlanta woman even claimed to be the owner of Nancy Hart's spinning wheel.

So then. The critics deflected, the legend soldiered on. By then it was already firmly part of the folklore; it could hardly do otherwise.

In 1912, the legend got a boost when railway workers preparing a bed for the Elberton and Eastern Railroad uncovered six skeletons near where the original Hart cabin was believed to have sat. These were immediately – and without any further recorded investigation or corroboration – taken as the bones of the Tories Nancy had captured and hanged.

This actually wasn't the first time that bones had been mentioned in connection with the Hart cabin. In his 1851 speech at Franklin College in which he first entered the lists to stir Nancy's legend, George Gilmer had noted that a 1795 freshet had unearthed bones under and around the Hart cabin. Gilmer made no clear connection, though, between these bones and Nancy's Tory prisoners. Like much of what he wrote, so much of what Gilmer said, on any subject, during his years in politics needs close examination – and often his pronouncements don't now bear up under it. (They didn't so much in his own time either.) Still, the 1851 claim and the 1912 finding, taken together, seem an odd coincidence. The finding of the six skeletons in 1912 certainly did nothing to hurt Nancy's legend, though.

As Coulter noted in 1955, through none of the growth of and the wrangling over the Nancy Hart legend did Henderson County, Kentucky, get on the bandwagon and make hay of its own connection with Nancy. Histories of the county written in the 1800s, he noted, did not mention her. Her son John appears in local records of the time but she does not. It wasn't until well into the 20th century that Nancy Hart's legend took root in the Bluegrass State, beginning with a DAR marker in Henderson County.

Georgia's success in ballyhooing Nancy Hart's stories into accepted history likely played no small part in this. In 1916, a painting of Nancy, commissioned by the Piedmont Continental Chapter of the DAR was presented to the state in a formal ceremony in the state capitol. Governor Nathaniel Harris accepted the painting and Lucien Lamar Knight, never unwilling to do his part in promoting Nancy, gave a suitably flowery speech on the legendary star of the hour: "What if her eyes were crossed? They were true enough to sentinel the Georgia forest in an hour of danger, and, like twin stars among the morning sky, were glorious enough to light the dawn of liberty."

The painting was placed in the State Department of Archives and History. Knight's speech, fortunately I think, had no such staying power and disappeared into newspaper morgues.

By this time, many things had been named for Nancy besides a county, its county seat, and a LaGrange women's militia company. The list included, in 1879, the naming of "The Nancy Hart," a locomotive that ran on the Hartwell Railroad, a branch off the main railway running between Elberton and Toccoa. In the 1920s, residents of Hartwell began a push for Congress to erect a monument honoring Nancy. This was finally realized in 1931, when the marker was unveiled. Georgia's celebrated U.S. Senator Richard B. Russell, Jr. gave the main address of the day. His speech included the story of Nancy capturing and hanging the five Tories. Later Elbert County would establish a park named for her, complete with a reconstructed cabin, on part of what had been the original Hart land. A section of Ga. 72 in Elbert County would also be named in her honor.

Now then. That's the story of how Nancy Hart's legend took root and grew. How much of it is true? Well, there was a woman named Nancy Hart and she did live near the Broad River in what's now Elbert County, Georgia, in the 1770s. After that, the truth is anyone's guess. There were indeed women who played heroic parts in the great drama that was the American Revolution and that is no less true for the Georgia and Carolina backcountry than in other places. Maybe more true in the Georgia and Carolina backcountry, because of the nature of the backcountry war and the makeup of the rough-hewn, hardscrabble people involved.

So probably within the legend of Nancy Hart there is at least one kernel of truth – a fact of most legends – but exactly what it is, or its nature, is unlikely ever to be known. Any story of her might have been lost forever, though, but for some Milledgeville newspaper man who was looking for good copy on Revolutionary War times to mark the occasion of the Marquis de Lafayette's visit to town and had somehow heard some story of Nancy Hart. Other writers picked up on it and over the years added to Nancy's adventures. They were good stories in their time. They still are. All the stories, too, tell something about the times in which they were told. It really doesn't matter if somehow, by someone, the truth of Nancy Hart's revolutionary adventures, if any, has been swamped by the legend. That's almost an American tradition with our early heroic literature. After all, George Washington didn't really chop down a cherry tree or throw a dollar across a river as Parson Weems wrote, and Paul Revere's ride wasn't quite as dramatic as Longfellow made it out.

It all calls to mind the ending of the great Western film "The Man Who Shot Liberty Valance." The revered U.S. Senator Ransom Stoddard (Jimmy Stewart), who years before rode to high political office on the renown he gained for having stood up to and killed the notorious outlaw Liberty Valance (Lee Marvin), has just told a local newspaper editor that it was his now deceased friend Tom Doniphan (John Wayne) who actually shot Valance to save his (Stoddard's) life. The editor decides not to print senator's revelation.

"When the legend becomes truth," he says, "print the legend."

Reconstruction of Hart cabin in Elbert County's Nancy Hart Park

Nancy Hart Park, Elbert County
(Author photos)

# 2

# Ol' Dan Tucker Was A Fine Ol' (Real) Man

Down the end of a winding red dirt road in northeast Georgia's Elbert County, a spot of tangled woods hide the remains of a mystery that stretches all the way to central Ohio and into the far-flung reaches of American folk music.

The woods cover a point of land jutting out into Lake Russell and looking across the Savannah River to the South Carolina shore. The quiet is broken only by the songs of birds, the wind-rustle of the trees and the faint lapping of the water at the lakeshore. Amid the trees is a crude and crumbling tombstone that marks the last resting place of the Reverend Daniel Tucker.

Tucker, buried at the spot with his wife, owned much of the surrounding land from 1798 until his death in 1818. His plantation included the scrub pine-covered red hills surrounding his gravesite and the rich bottom lands covered now by the lake. The gravesite promontory overlooks the stretch of the river where Tucker operated a ferry on one of the main routes crossing the Savannah in the years before the upper river was bridged. For decades afterward, until the lake finally covered the area in the early 1980s, the area was known as Tucker's Ferry.

In the lore of Elbert County (and indeed according to several historians today) the Rev. Tucker was the "Ol' Dan Tucker" of song and legend. What songs! And what a legend! He was the "fine ol' man" who "washed his face in a fryin' pan" and "combed his hair with a wagon wheel," among other feats. According to lore, the popular tunes about Tucker originated among his slaves, who according to accounts of the day, held Tucker in high regard (a notion unpopular in modern times, but not altogether unknown in the historical record).

The story of the Reverend Tucker is unchallenged in Elbert County. It is deeply etched in the county's lore and written into local history as fact. The state historical marker about eight miles east of Elberton on Ga. 72 that points passersby to Tucker's grave even gives the story an official stamp of approval.

State historical marker on Ga. 72, approximately eight miles east of Elberton (author photo)

## A Different Story

The folks in Knox County, Ohio, though, tell a different story. They credit the "Ol' Dan Tucker" song to their own native son, Daniel Decatur Emmett, the composer and minstrel performer who is also credited with composing the Southern anthem "Dixie" in 1859.

Knox County local history holds that young Emmett – a born musician – taught himself very early to play the fiddle and showed a talent for composing his own tunes. Local lore has him performing "Ol' Dan Tucker" for the first time at the July 4th celebration in his hometown of Mount Vernon in 1830, when he was just fifteen years old. He is said to have arrived at the name of the song's subject by combining his own name (Daniel) with that of his dog, "Tucker."[1]

The situation perplexes historians. Are either of the stories actually based in fact? If yes, then which? Is it even possible now to know the truth? Any search for the answers to this historical puzzle has to begin with the two Daniels themselves.

## Which Daniel?

Daniel Tucker was born February 14, 1740 in Amelia County, Virginia, one of thirteen children of Daniel and Elizabeth Clay Tucker. His was a branch of the Tucker family that was one of the most distinguished of Virginia, tracing its origins in the colony back to the very founding.

The first Tuckers in America – the brothers George and Daniel Tucker – were scions of England's landed gentry and original members of the Virginia Company. They had sailed in 1606 to help found what became the colony at Jamestown. This earlier Daniel Tucker, as an army captain in the service of King James I, was later appointed a royal governor of Bermuda. The family's lineage also included the renowned colonial jurist St. George Tucker of Williamsburg.[2] The family branched far and wide in the colonies, and in the years before the American Revolution some of the Tuckers had reached northeast Georgia. A George Tucker, one of our Daniel's cousins, arrived in 1774 to take up a claim in the Georgia lands ceded by the Cherokee and Creek in exchange in exchange for an accumulated trade debt, lands along the Savannah River between the Little and Tugaloo Rivers and extending westward nearly to the Oconee River. George would eventually come to serve in the Georgia militia under Elijah Clarke and take part in the rebel victory over a loyalist force at Kettle Creek on February 14, 1779.[3]

By the time of the Revolution, Daniel Tucker was himself moving southward. He had at some point traveled to Wake County, North Carolina, either together with or to join his parents and some of his siblings. By that time he had married Frances Epps, a distant cousin from Dinwiddie County, Virginia. During the Revolution, Tucker served variously with the 2nd, the 6th and the 8th North Carolina regiments, rising to the rank of captain.

After the Revolution, Tucker was ordained as a Methodist minister. He was described as "the Rev. Daniel Tucker" for the first time in the records of a land sale in Mecklenburg County, Virginia, in which he sold lands as an agent for this father. When, even roughly, Daniel moved to Georgia is uncertain, but it was probably not before his father's death in Wake County in 1792.[4]

In 1798, he purchased his property in Elbert County, amid the landed gentry such as the local Revolutionary War hero Stephen Heard, from whom he purchased the ferry tract. Many were, like Heard, from Tucker's own original area of Virginia, some likely kin, all of whom had settled in the fertile upper Savannah River valley. It was an area destined to prosper in the years after the war, well within a day's ride of the developing riverport of Petersburg, which as a main shipping point for tobacco and other commodities to Augusta and Savannah would grow to be for a time Georgia's third largest city. Here the reverend built his home, "Point Lookout," and prospered as a planter and ferry owner.

According to recollections that passed into lore, the Rev. Tucker was popular with the slaves, not only his own but those of his neighbors as well. In the 1940s, Herbert Wilcox, a noted local journalist in Elbert County as well as a correspondent for both the *Atlanta Journal-Constitution* and the *Atlanta Journal-Constitution Magazine*, interviewed a

Mrs. Guy Rucker, whose great-grandfather had reportedly been a friend and neighbor of Tucker. The reverend was popular among the slaves, according to Mrs. Rucker's account, because he spent a great deal of time preaching to and praying with them. This, she said, led them to make up the songs of which Tucker was the main actor.[5]

Tucker died April 7, 1818 at the age of seventy-eight. Even though he was of an age, especially for the times, when his death might be attributed to simple "old age," local lore has him dying as the result of a mishap. According to the tales, Tucker died either of snakebite or of injuries resulting from his horse throwing him after it was bitten. Either version could offer some clue of the mysterious death attributed to him in the songs – "… died with a toothache in his heel."

**The Man From Ohio**

Daniel Decatur Emmett spent his first seventeen years in his years in his native Mt. Vernon, Ohio, but his musical ambitions led him elsewhere. In 1832, he joined the U.S. Army and became the lead fifer in the post band of Jefferson Barracks, Missouri. He was discharged three years later when authorities learned he had lied about his age at enlistment.

He joined a series of circus bands – very popular at the time – in which he played the fiddle and learned and perfected the then popular art of performing in black face, acting according to black stereotypes. It was a common, and very popular, theme of performances in all regions of the United States that would endure well into the first decades of the 20th century.

In the 1840s, Emmett joined with three other performers in creating the group "Old Virginia Minstrels." The quartet, in costume and black face, played tunes with the banjo, fiddle, bones and tambourine. Emmett contributed several songs to the group's repertoire, including one he called "Ol' Dan Tucker."

Emmett was working with a minstrel troupe in New York City in the winter of 1859 when he introduced a new song "Dixie," a catchy tune that would soon be embraced as an unofficial anthem by the seceding South. According to the most accepted version of the now famous tune's origin, the bitter cold winters of the northeastern states led Emmett to think of what was a common expression among circus performers, who preferred to tour in the warmer, or at least less cold, South during the winter months: "I wish I was in the land of cotton … away down South in Dixie."

Emmett was a staunch Unionist, but after the war, ironically, he found his greatest popularity as a minstrel touring the reconstructing South. He continued to tour until 1895, when at the age of 80 he retired back to his hometown, dying there in 1904.[6]

**Emmett whistled (and sung) "Dixie" but did he write it?**

An examination of the origin of one of Emmett's best known tunes may well cast some light on the origins of the other.

"It turns out that "Dixie" was actually written by a former slave living in Ohio," said Ron Pen, director of the John Jacob Niles Center for American Music at the University of Kentucky.[7]

Indeed, a respectable body of thought among musicologists maintains that "Dixie" may have originated with Ben and Lew Snowden, members of a black family that moved to Clinton, Ohio, in Emmett's own native Knox County, years before the Civil War. The Snowden family performed banjo and fiddle tunes for both black and white audiences throughout central Ohio during the antebellum years.[8]

What are the odds that Emmett might have come by "Ol' Dan Tucker" the same way?

Very good, as it turns out. If the tune was in circulation enough that Emmett could have heard it, anywhere he happened to be, at anytime, then it was up for grabs. The tune is attributed to Emmett, according to Pen, "only because he had it published … As with 'Dixie,' it is probably that he put it in the form that was most recognizable and he had it notated and printed and published."

"Ol' Dan Tucker," said Pen, "was probably a song that passed through the fiddle tune/hoedown oral tradition until it reached Emmett and was spread through the minstrels where it became wildly successful."

Both tunes share the characteristics of having multiple versions, which Pen describes as an earmark of folk music. That is especially true of "Ol' Dan Tucker," which now has many more verses than those published by Emmett, with some versions and verses being regional.

"Songs like this are a magnet for 'floating couplets,' said Pen, "in which nonsensical, non-chronological verses are linked together through a skeleton of melodic framework and a central theme or character of the song."

While these very traits of folk music can obscure its origins, Pen said, they certainly don't at all rule out that "Ol' Dan Tucker" could have originated just as Elbert County lore holds it did.

All of which means that the mystery surrounding "Ol' Dan Tucker" must remain just that – a mystery, unsolved, with any solution hidden in the mists of time.

Emmett could have made it all up himself – taking his own and his dog's names – or he could have borrowed it from early black folk music, as he is alleged to have done with "Dixie." Perhaps the only people who ever knew the answer to the puzzle of "Ol' Dan Tucker" lie in the several slave graveyards not very far from Tucker's own grave.

The enduring mystery of "Ol' Dan Tucker" means that Knox County, Ohio, and Elbert County, Georgia, can both hold on to their pieces of the legend for as long as the old song is sung.

The grave of "ol' Dan Tucker" of song and legend? The grave lies a few miles off Ga. 72, about seven miles east of Elberton. Tucker once owned the surrounding lands.

The headstone of the
Rev. Daniel Tucker
(Author photos)

# 3

# The Tragedy of Beverly Allen

On January 11, 1794, Beverly Allen raised a flintlock pistol and fired through the door of an Augusta boarding house. The lead pistol ball tore through the wood and entered the head of U.S. Marshal Robert Forsyth, killing him on the spot.

The drama of the scene is difficult to overstate. The Scottish-born Forsyth had served with distinction in the American Revolution, was in fact an acquaintance of President George Washington. He was a man who had taken the reins of civic leadership in the Augusta community, among other things serving as a trustee of a local academy. A man on the rise in the new republic. All that prospect had now ended in a pool of blood on the boarding house floor. Beverly Allen was also a man of some distinction. Or had been. Not so long before he had been one of the best known and lauded ministers of the Methodist church, his star also on the rise. Until his fall from grace. Now he was notorious, soon to be hunted, left to live the rest of his life, as we know from accounts of his end, believing that he was beyond all redemption.

Just over two years before, Beverly Allen, then about thirty-six years old, had been defrocked from the Methodist ministry after an eleven-year career that had witnessed his rapid climb to the upper rungs of his church. Throughout the Carolinas and Georgia he had earned the reputation as a powerful and charismatic preacher who held congregations in the palm of his hand. He also had a reputation, earned or not, among the Methodist Church leaders as a prideful man who would readily challenge their authority, and perhaps even relished doing so.

By the time he was defrocked he also had the whispered reputation in church circles of a notorious rake. According to gossip he had abandoned wife and family and perpetrated some damning scandal during his last ministry on Edisto Island, near Charleston, South Carolina. Of that, it seems, rumors are all that there are.

That is because the purported scandal evidently shocked the Methodist Church hierarchy to its core, with the details remaining a mystery because no one with knowledge of the sordid facts apparently ever felt comfortable committing them to paper and posterity. All that was set down were dark hints of seduction. Whatever the reason for his being turned out of the church, Beverly ended up joining his brother William in Elbert County.

Forsyth and two deputies had tried to serve papers on the two brothers, documents calling them to account for debts contracted as part of the mercantile and tavern they ran in Elbert County, monies now past due. What moved Beverly Allen to flee to his room to avoid service of the papers and then turn to kill the pursuing Forsyth died with him over twenty years later. It's not recorded that he ever offered his reasons.

Beverly Allen's silence left a void for a legend to fill.

For ironically, his shooting of Forsyth elevated Beverly Allen to a celebrated notoriety in Elbert County comparable perhaps to the legendary Robin Hood or the later anti-hero (to some) outlaw Jesse James. Not once but twice Allen escaped from jail with the help of friends and, apparently, his brother's associates and likely political cronies. The second jailbreak, in fact, seems to have happened with the help of a mob that included some of Elbert County's leading citizens.

Some circumstances surrounding this indicate that the brothers' troubles – and Beverly's rescue – involved the rough-and-tumble of local factional politics, which would indeed go a long way toward an explanation. It certainly would have fit the character of the times.

Beverly fled to Kentucky, to an area there known at the time as a refuge for outlaws. He had arrived in Elbert County troubled by his past and his personal demons. He had reached the pinnacle of his calling and then had been brought low by, it seems, his personal foibles perhaps tinged with church politics. In Kentucky, he forged a new life, recovered his family, and evidently prospered. But it brought him no peace. By reliable accounts, he died tormented by his past, haunted still by his demons and in terror of facing hellfire for his sins. But his legend lived on in north Georgia. In Elbert County lore it lives still.

## The Rise

Beverly Anthony Allen is believed to have been born in Spotsylvania County, Virginia, in 1757 into the upper rank of the yeoman farmer class. William, also figuring prominently in our tale, is believed to have been born a year earlier in Amherst County, Virginia. Accounts indicate that there was also a third brother, Reuben, and at least one sister.[1]

In 1778, just before his first known affiliation with the Methodist Church, records indicate that Beverly was a practicing physician in Talbot County, Maryland. He would have been only twenty-one years old, but his youth would not have ruled out his being a doctor in those times. A practical education in the state of the medical art of the late 18th century in the American colonies could often be gained by apprenticeship to an older, experienced doctor, beginning perhaps when the young apprentice was as young as fifteen. Still, Beverly's apparent achievement at such an age speaks to extraordinary ability.

How the young doctor first fell under the sway of the church remains uncertain, but by 1782 he was a full-fledged minister of the Methodist Church, preaching first in Maryland and then in North Carolina. From the beginning this young man of the cloth showed charm and power as a speaker, which helped him overcome the obstacles and prejudices ministers of the new denomination encountered in the Methodist church's early years.

Indeed, charm and bearing were his hallmarks. One observer described Allen as a "brilliant young preacher of striking appearance and unusual popularity... He could win his way wherever he went and gain a bearing among all."[2] Another observer, Mrs. William Cole, of his church in Salisbury, North Carolina in 1783 favored future followers of his story by leaving this fuller impression of him:

"Soon after my return to Salisbury, at the close of the [Revolutionary] war, it was announced that there would be preaching in a schoolhouse by a new kind of people, called Methodists... I went early expecting to see a minister resembling the old parsons; but judge of my surprise, when instead of a stout, good looking, finely dressed gentleman with gown and supplice, in silk stockings and silver buckles, in walked a slender, delicate young man, dressed in homespun cotton jeans. Though plainly attired, I perceived in his countenance unusual solemnity and goodness. The impressions made upon my mind and heart by this sermon — the first I ever heard from a Methodist minister — have never been effaced from my memory. The subject was experimental religion, explained and enforced. To my surprise, the preacher unfolded my experience, and seemed to give in detail all the exercises of my mind, from my first conviction for sin, until I was made happy in the love of God. Not till then did I know that I enjoyed religion; although happy, I did not fully understand why. My experience exactly agreeing with the word preached, I concluded that the preacher, an entire stranger, could not have known so much about me, had not God revealed it to him. At his third visit he formed a small class, of which I was one. ..."[3]

Allen's rise to acclaim was by all indications rapid. He was not at the Christmastime 1784 conference of the church leadership in Baltimore, at which the Methodist Episcopal Church was organized, but his prominence was such that the gathering elected one of the church's original twelve elders.

Francis Asbury, considered the founding father of American Methodism, was a man who brooked no challenges to his way of governing the church or following church doctrine, but Beverly Allen was, it seems, even by the time of his election as an elder showing a determination to go his own way. In Asbury's correspondence from shortly after the Baltimore conference he is already speaking of Allen as "a promising young man, but a bit of a Dissenter."[4]

We can only speculate on Allen's reasons for being a maverick. Perhaps his rapid rise within the church led the young man of the cloth to fall into the very sin of pride that he likely admonished from time to time in his sermons. After all, in just short of three years he had gone from minister to church elder, his abilities in the pulpit obvious to all, no less, it seems safe to suppose, obvious to himself. We're also on safe ground, it view of his later history, to suppose that he was arrogant, headstrong, mercurial, maybe even unstable, as Asbury was to claim. In Baltimore though, his ability to hold the spiritually seeking spellbound outweighed any quibbles about his tendencies toward waywardness.

In any case, we know that the relationship between Asbury and Allen grew worse as time unspooled. Years later, after Allen's fall from grace and shooting of Forsyth, Asbury commented in his private journal: "Poor Beverly Allen ... has been going from bad to worse these seven or eight years, speaking against me to preachers and people and writing to Mr. [John] Wesley and Dr. [Thomas] Coke, and being thereby the source of most of the mischief that has followed."[5]

In the spring of 1785, Asbury dispatched the newly invested elder to Georgia, with the whole state his circuit. Why Asbury chose Georgia as Allen's next ministry is unclear, but Methodist Church historian Duane Maxey, citing Asbury's letters and journal entries, speculates that Georgia was intended as a sort of exile for the troublesome pastor. Similarly, it's also not known for certain if Beverly Allen already had at least some connection with Georgia through William. It is fairly certain that William had been in Georgia by some circumstance for some time, likely some years, before Beverly first ventured there. William's reasons, though, had nothing to do with circuit riding and everything to do with settling a new land.

A William Allen appears in Georgia records for the first time in 1774, on the rolls of the enlisted men of the rangers assigned to Fort James. This fort was built and garrisoned at the confluence of the Broad and Savannah Rivers on the orders of Georgia's royal governor James Wright to protect settlers and keep the King's peace in the upper Savannah River valley lands between the Little and Tugaloo Rivers. This tract had been obtained by the British Crown in 1773 from the Creek and Cherokee tribes in payment for trading debts owed traders and Savannah and Charleston merchants.[6]

It's unclear, however, whether this is our William Allen. Beverly's older brother, however, did serve in a company of the Georgia line that served in the Augusta area during the revolution. There were two William Allens in these companies, according to records, one most likely also the William Allen who served at Fort James. Some recruiting for Georgia line companies was done in eastern and central Virginia, so the unresolved question reduces to when our William Allen first came to Georgia. His choosing to settle in the new lands opened in 1773 perhaps hints at a familiarity from having served as a ranger at Fort James. The upper reaches of the Savannah River valley that Beverly Allen probably visited for the first time in early 1785 was a more unsettled and rough-and-tumble place than he likely had experienced till then in Maryland or eastern and coastal North Carolina. His time in Georgia now would not be long, but in the ironic way fate often twists the area was to play a key role in his destiny.

If Georgia was intended to be an exile for Beverly Allen, evidently he wasn't long in regaining some favor. Within a few months, Thomas Coke, in time the Methodist Church's first bishop but during this time directing the church's missions, sent Allen to minister in Charleston, South Carolina. Some sources have Allen given the post in Charleston in 1787, but he was there at least long enough in 1785 to meet and woo his future wife, because in February 1786 he married Anna Singletary, the youngest daughter of John Singletary, a plantation owner with substantial holdings on the Wappoo River below Charleston.[7]

Early on, Allen seems to have set out on his new ministry with all the confidence born of his impressive record, sure he would shepherd converts into the Church. "The field seemed white unto the harvest, as the people are ready to hear the word," he wrote Asbury. "Many hundreds flocked to hear the word of the Lord and many seemed truly awakened."[8]

Charleston, however, was a far different place than Allen had ever ministered before. A major American port since colonial times, larger than Wilmington where Allen had at one time ministered, Charleston was not only a more urbane and worldly place than Allen had perhaps ever experienced but it was also an old city, long a solid stronghold of the Anglican Church even after a large infusion of French Huguenot influence. (Most Huguenots who immigrated to the South Carolina Low Country in time became strong Anglicans, even Anglicizing their names.) Before long Allen was writing to Asbury: "The people seem afraid to hear us, lest they should be infected with Methodism, which they deem as dangerous as the plague."[9] By the end of 1786, though, he was reporting some success. He had a committed congregation of over thirty members, with plans to build a church sanctuary on Charleston's Cumberland Street.

In 1791, Coke sent Allen to take over the mission on Edisto Island, a coastal island planter community near Charleston. Just before taking up his new post, Allen mailed a manuscript to John Wesley, Methodism's founder living in England, a narrative of his successes in Georgia and South Carolina. It is a remarkable piece to have been written by a man of the cloth whom one would think would include piety and humility among his stock in trade. It drips with the pride Allen's maverick record and Asbury's known misgivings lead one to think Allen had shown in past years. In writing of his success in drawing converts, for example, he compares himself to Nehemiah, Biblical founder of the temple. The narrative would appear in a 1792 edition of *Arminian Magazine* as "Some Account of the Work of the Lord in America," but by the time it was published Beverly Allen was no longer a minister. Nothing is recorded about Allen's ministry on Edisto Island, but it was there that the mystery of Beverly Allen's fall from grace began.

### The Fall

The minutes of the Methodist Church's 1792 conference read simply "Expelled from connection: Beverly Allen." That's all. No details as to why. No details of Beverly Allen's misdeeds were set down in any church record or, so far as can be found, any private letter or journal. In the 1830s, theological historian Nathan Bangs simply said, "In the notice we have taken of the rise and progress of Methodism in Charleston, South Carolina, we have seen that Mr. Allen brought a great reproach upon the Church in that place by his apostasy. What the particular sin was by which he thus wounded the cause of God, I am not informed."[10]

In more recent times, church historian Maxey has cited letters referring only to Allen's expulsion "for immorality" and a "flagrant crime." From a time when some even venal moral transgressions were crimes, even the juxtaposition of the two terms in description offer little help. The apparent seriousness of Allen's actions in the Church's eyes, however, bring most speculation on the nature of his offense around to thinking it was most likely adultery. Whatever the reason, Beverly Allen left Charleston, leaving his wife and young family behind.

### On The Run

The now disgraced Beverly next appeared in Elbert County, where he joined William in the latter's business enterprises. William had acquired a large tract of land along Beaverdam Creek in the eastern part of the county and operated a mercantile, a tavern and a grist mill near a creek ford on a road from an upper Savannah River crossing to the bustling town of Petersburg, further down river.

Petersburg had developed near the site of old Fort James, where in the last years of colonial times the royal governor had planned a never-built town to be called Dartmouth, and was now on its way to eventually become for a time Georgia's third largest city. It was the main riverport for shipping tobacco and other commodities downriver to Augusta and Savannah, and was just upriver from a main crossing of the Savannah River for travelers and freight haulers from South Carolina.

Lots in this town on the bloom were at a premium, and by the time Beverly joined William the older brother had prospered enough to own several. William was also prominent enough to have been elected a captain in the local militia, a status usually granted to the most civilly active up-and-comers in a community. It was a status and circumstance that would later prove of no small importance in saving Beverly from the hangman's noose.

By late 1793, perhaps partly in fallout from the economic realignments and the uncertainties of that time in the new American republic, the Allen brothers had overextended themselves and creditors in Augusta had named them in several lawsuits. In a time of little hard money, credit was everything. It was during a trip to Augusta to try to settle some of these debts that Allen encountered Forsyth.

Nothing substantial is recorded about the weather in Augusta on Saturday, January 11, 1794, but it's not much of a reach to suppose the day was cold, possibly rainy. It's not known when the Allens arrived in Augusta after what was even in the best of weather at least an exhausting two and one-half day ride from the banks of Beaverdam Creek. But they took a room at the boarding house owned by a Mrs. Dixon. It was a well-known establishment, with a good reputation, and would eventually become a local landmark – and be washed of any stain of notoriety stemming from this day – when George Washington would stay there while visiting Augusta on his farewell tour after leaving the presidency. It was here that Robert Forsyth and his two deputies found William and Beverly Allen.

According to an account published in the local newspaper, the *Augusta Chronicle*, one week later, the lawmen approached the brothers, who were talking with acquaintances, and asked to speak with them privately. The newspaper account opined that Forsyth wished to spare the Allens the embarrassment of being publicly served with summonses. There are two different versions of the events that followed, according to the newspaper account. One is that William Allen accepted service while Beverly fled to their second floor room. The other version has both brothers fleeing. If William had accepted service of the papers, there would hardly have been a reason for Forsyth to pursue, so it seems likely that both fled to their room.

Whichever of the openings to the drama is true, witnesses attested that when Forsyth approached the room, Beverly warned him through the closed door that if he came any further he would blow the marshal's brains out. Beverly then fired, the pistol ball going through the door and hitting Forsyth in the head, the wound immediately fatal.

The then thirty-nine-year-old Forsyth had been a U.S. marshal for nearly five years, one of the thirteen original federal marshals (one for each state) appointed in 1789 by President George Washington. Born in Scotland in 1754, Forsyth had come to America with his father and lived in New England until moving to Fredericksburg, Virginia around 1774. Two years later, he enlisted in the colonial forces and, in 1779, was commissioned a captain in the light dragoons. Eventually, Forsyth transferred to the commissary department of the Continental Army's Southern Department and ended the war as a major in the First Virginia Legion.

In 1785, he had moved his family from Fredericksburg to Augusta. He quickly rose in his new community, becoming a county commissioner and a trustee of a school as well as working as a tax assessor and justice of the peace before Washington appointed him as a

U.S. marshal. He was a merchant, a farmer, and a member of the Augusta Masonic lodge. He left a widow and two sons. He was buried in the cemetery of St. Paul's Episcopal Church in Augusta.[11]

Both Allens were arrested for Forsyth's murder, but a coroner's inquest charged just Beverly with the crime. He was held in the Richmond County jail, the gallows his almost certain fate. When the news reached Elbert County, the brothers' friends immediately rallied to his support. They devised a desperate strategy to get him off: They would seek to have him declared insane.

It was a piece of attempted legal legerdemain that amused Beverly's old adversary Francis Asbury when he learned of it. (Asbury seemed more concerned, however, how Beverly's woes might reflect on the Methodist Church.)

"The masterpiece of all, is," Asbury wrote in his journal, "a petition is prepared declaring him to have shown marks of insanity previous to his killing the major! The poor Methodists also must unjustly be put to the rack on his account, although he has been expelled from among us these two years. I have had my opinion of him these nine years; and gave Dr. Coke my thoughts of him before his ordination. I pity, I pray for him, that, if his life be given up to justice, his soul may yet be saved."[12]

The effort to prove that Beverly Allen was insane showed no real signs of working. (Not holding the obviously insane legally accountable for their actions did have some precedent in English common law, however.) So six weeks after the shooting, he escaped from the Richmond County jail, reportedly with the aid of a bribed guard. Rewards were immediately offered for Allen's recapture. "The apprehension of this man will be liberally rewarded by the respected inhabitants of Augusta," the announcement in the March 1 edition of the *Augusta Chronicle* read, "besides the approving voice of every good character in America."

Allen sought refuge from his brother in Elbert County. The fugitive was finally located and recaptured, however, on June 15. This time, his supporters and William's militia comrades rallied to his aid by more direct means.

Two weeks later, William Barnett, a justice of the peace in Elbert County, wrote Georgia Governor George Mathews about the events: "On the 15th instant the sheriff of this County with myself an several others went to the house of Mr. William Allen where we had reason to believe that Beverly Allen who had escaped from Richmond County Gaol, was concealed. We accordingly found him very ingeniously secreted in the garratt of the house of Wm. Allen. We carried him from thence to our gaol. In about two hours after our arrival we were surprised by an armed force to the amount of some thirty odd, headed by Wm. Allen whose intentions he said were to protect Beverly Allen from Insults and from being carried to Augusta, though for some cause best known to themselves, they Retreated without any further molestation."

Barnett called for reinforcements from the militia, likely aware of William's ties with the organization but perhaps feeling there was no other choice. Two days later, about forty or fifty armed men with blackened faces arrived at the jail. Badly outnumbered, the officer in charge ordered his men to hold fire.

"The mob advanced and rescued the prisoner," Barnett informed the governor. "We have on slight testimony apprehended four of the party two of which were Militia Captains. It is extraordinary to think of the influence this man has had on the minds of the citizens of this County. I think they are a majority in his favor."

Barnett ended his narrative by telling Mathews that he was outlining the facts of the incident "should your excellency think it worthy of an Executive interference we should be happy to receive any such assistance as you might think proper to give."[13]

What, if any, personal, political or business connection that Mathews, who hailed from the Oglethorpe County area, just southwest of Elbert, might have had with the Allen brothers, especially Willam, isn't known. But there is no record that the governor ever offered any "interference".

In seeking every avenue in the attempt to bring Beverly Allen to justice and an eventual appointment with a hangman, Barnett might have had personal motives as well as any sense of duty as a justice of the peace. He had, in fact, been a close friend of Robert Forsyth, having been both a tax collector and sheriff in Richmond County before moving to Elbert County in 1790.

He and William Allen had also clashed in local politics and would again. In 1795, he would be among William Allen's opponents for an election of local delegates to a state constitutional convention. William Allen would go on to serve in several elected offices, including, perhaps ironically, justice of the peace.

So far as is known, however, after his escape Beverly left Georgia for good.


**Refuge, But Not Redemption**

Kentucky in the middle 1790s was nearly the edge of the frontier, with some parts of it far more dangerous with human inhabitants than it had been as uncharted wilderness.

Logan County was such a place, being at that time a refuge for outlaws of all stripes. Peter Cartwright, himself a future Methodist minister of acclaim, described in his memoirs the place to which his father moved their family in 1793.

"Logan County, when my father moved to it, was called 'Rogues' Harbor,'" Cartwright recalled. "Here many refugees, from almost all parts of the Union, fled to escape justice or punishment; for although there was law, yet it could not be executed, and it was a desperate state of society. Murderers, horse thieves, highway robbers, and counterfeiters fled here until they combined and actually formed a majority."[14]

It was a natural place of the time for the former minister-turned-fugitive to finally go to ground. In such a place any forces of the law seldom ventured. At least for a time. Later, a regulator movement, as had developed on the frontiers of North and South Carolina, would dampen the enthusiasm of the lawless and open the way for law and order and all their trappings, but in 1794 it offered just the kind of shelter Beverly Allen sought.

He was evidently never molested in the years that followed, despite his past being something of an open secret. He practiced medicine again and took in boarding students at least on occasion. Peter Cartwright in his early teens was one of his students but found him a poor teacher. He was, according to Cartwright, "not well-qualified to teach correctly, and I made but small progress. I, however, learned to read, write, and cipher a little, but very imperfectly."[15]

Allen's wife and family joined him, and at some point his brother Rueben and their sister also settled in Logan County. (The sister, according to Cartwright, married a local tavern keeper.) His and his wife's family would grow to nine children and he prospered, perhaps helped by capital from his wife's inheritance.

By 1804, he had settled in the Green River valley, near Russellville, in time acquiring and farming nearly one thousand acres and building a water-powered sawmill.

The new life in the new land did not bring him peace, though. He abandoned the Methodist faith for Universalism, Methodism's near polar opposite. He returned to the Methodist Church on his deathbed, but still believed redemption beyond his reach.

Peter Cartwright, by then a minister such as Allen might have been, fortuitously was with Allen when he died in Logan County in 1816: "It fell to my lot, after I had been a preacher several years, to visit the doctor on his dying bed. I talked to, and prayed with him. Just before he died I asked him if he was willing to die and meet his final Judge with his Universalist sentiments. He frankly said he was not. He said he could make the mercy of God cover every case in his mind but his own, but he thought there was no mercy for him; and in this state of mind he left the world, bidding his family and friends an eternal farewell, warning them not to come to that place of torment to which he felt himself eternally doomed."[16]

Allen's wife lived on in Logan County until her death in 1850, gradually, by most accounts, slipping into poverty, in her last years taken in and cared for by a neighbor. She was buried beside her husband in the Allen cemetery in Dot. Kentucky. Allen's crumbling tombstone is barely legible.

Robert Forsyth's sons fulfilled their father's lost promise. His son John served Georgia as a U.S. representative, a U.S. senator, as the state's thirty-third governor and was U.S. Secretary of State during the administration of Andrew Jackson. Both Forsyth County and the city of Forsyth are named in John Forsyth's honor.

In 1981, the U.S. Marshals Service created the "Robert Forsyth Act of Valor Award." The award is given to a U.S. Marshals Service employee who demonstrates unusual courage, good judgment, and competence in hostile circumstances, or who has performed an act or service which saved the life of another person while endangering his/her own life.

In 1997, Governor Zell Miller dedicated the Georgia Public Safety Memorial at the Public Safety Training Center in Forsyth. The monument memorializes Georgia law enforcement officers, firefighters, corrections officers, emergency medical technicians and emergency management agency personnel who lose their lives in the line of duty. The first name carved on the memorial is that of Robert Forsyth.

# 4

# "Doc" Tommy Scott, Georgia's Merry Minstrel

"Doc" Tommy Scott in his memorabilia room (author photo)

The slim, wiry man glowed with the pure joy of life itself. It was hard to believe that he had passed his ninety-fifth birthday and has spent the better part of eight decades on a stage. Somewhere. Just hours before, he had driven his motor home over the mountains to his Eastanollee, Georgia, home from Owensboro, Kentucky, where he had appeared at a festival honoring the one hundredth birthday of one of his oldest friends, the late bluegrass legend Bill Monroe.

"Doc" Tommy Scott and his famous medicine show no longer travel America's highways and byways but he is nowhere near ready to leave the road. He has worn out ten motor homes in his life, racking up untold miles, but number eleven "has a lot of good miles in her yet."

Georgia's merry minstrel, in one way or the other Tommy Scott has known the whole world as his stage.

His first real job in music came at seventeen, when he left home to travel with a medicine show. That was in 1934. In time came regular work performing with other musicians on radio, then his own shows and albums, his own traveling shows and then, finally, his legendary "Doc Tommy Scott's Last Real Old Time Medicine Show". Along the way he's written over three hundred songs, appeared in over twenty-five movies with the likes of early matinee idol "Sunset" Carson, and befriended and shared the stage with most of the legends of bluegrass and country and western music.

In his lifetime, by his reckoning, he's played about 30,000 towns: "Often going seven days a week for about eighty years." In the years when he, his late wife, Frankie, and his medicine show performers were on the open road, the merry band would head out right after New Years Day and get back to Eastanollee just before Thanksgiving.

These days he's at his home outside Eastanollee more often than not. From the outside, the house, reached down a country road, looks like the world's most sprawling Chinese restaurant, and most of the rooms inside show a definite Oriental motif. "The house was Frankie's idea," he explained. "I told her to do it up any way she wanted." One room, though, is his, a packed museum of his life onstage. It tells a story of country and western music as both a profession and a performed art. The music is part of the story of the rural American soul. It's the music of front porches and country dances. It's the theme of Tommy Scott's story.

Nearly every inch of the walls and even part of the ceiling of the room are covered with artifacts and memorabilia. Posters from his many movies. Posters from his medicine show. Photographs of Scott with other celebrities. With "Tonight Show" host Johnny Carson. With Oprah Winfrey. With country music impresario Ralph Emery. With famed journalist Charles Kuralt. With comedian and late night television host David Letterman. Even with the hosts of a Russian television show who ventured all the way from Moscow to interview Scott in his front yard.

Many photographs show him with old friends such as Western movie star Tim McCoy and country music legend David "Stringbean" Ackeman. Still photographs from some scenes out of the "Saturday afternoon Western"-style movies he appeared in, such as "The Guns of Obadiah Crawford," line one wall. Framed letters from fans who have lived in the White House have their place. The letter from the office of President Richard Nixon is signed by Nixon's secretary Rosemary Woods, who gained her own fame in political history over eighteen minutes of missing audiotape. Props from his medicine show are here and there. Front and center is a pair of his trademark shiny red top hats.

Scott gazed around the room with a look of pride and wonder. "There's a lot of work and a lot of history in this room," he said. "But I've had a lot of fun over the years."

### Son Of Georgia's Red Clay Hills

Tommy Scott was born June 24, 1917, the first child of Clifton Scott and Elizabeth "Lizzie" Collins Scott, on their farm at Eastanollee, just outside Toccoa. Nine years later would follow his sister, Cleo, his first performing partner. The Scotts were small farmers, had been for generations, and from an early age, he would later set down in his memoirs, Tommy Scott knew in his heart his father that wanted him to continue the tradition of scratching his living from the red Georgia soil.

Early on, though, the young Tommy discovered a passion for drawing and painting and, in time, for music. Music was as much a part of rural life of his childhood as the long rows of cotton on which the family's cash money for the year depended. The land fed the people, but music, "hillbilly music," as Scott would always call it, helped sustain their souls.

That's how it had been for as far back as anyone could remember, as far back as the first Scot-Irish settlers clawing out their place in the world in the southern Appalachian Mountains and lower hill country. Not only had the music soothed the wounds of the hard life it had also carried the echoes of the Scottish highlands and glens and the green hills of Ireland, homelands only their great-great grandparents, perhaps, had ever seen.

Whenever people gathered, he remembered, "someone always brought out fiddles and guitars." In time, he would join them. "When I was ten years old, I made my first public appearance in a fiddling contest, which whet my taste for more and more music. I kept playing and writing my own songs, sure that one day I would be a performer."

With six dollars saved by the nickel and dime at a time he bought his first guitar at a pawn shop and learned to play it. His sister, Cleo, six years old by this time, also learned to play it on the sly, sneaking his treasured instrument out when he was at school. (When she was seven, she was given her one of her own.) Tommy was soon playing at cake walks and other affairs for a few coins and later he and Cleo performed regularly on WTFI, a radio station set up in the basement of the Presbyterian church in Toccoa.

"We often went to the radio station and sang and played our hillbilly music over the air," Tommy remembered. "They were glad to have us, and I suspect it greatly encouraged my desire to work around music, whether it was writing songs or playing the guitar."

Radio, in fact, from its commercial beginning in 1920, had created a world in which Tommy Scott would later thrive. It had pulled country music out of the community square dances and other amateur venues and given the talented and the passionate a wider audience. The beckoning star, of course, was the Grand Ol' Opry, which began broadcasting from Nashville in 1925. That was a long way from the small community radio station in the church basement, but on April 1, 1933, the fifteen-year-old Tommy took his next step, appearing on a show from WAIM in Anderson, S.C.

The love of drawing and painting remained, however, and his high school teachers encouraged him to consider it for his life's work. But Tommy knew he wanted to play his music. His parents as always seemed to have "soft hearts" toward his wanting to draw or play music, despite the desires he was sure his father had for Tommy to work the land as he did. But there also seemed to be something else that made his father understand the young Tommy. "I suspect," Scott would later write in his memoirs, "it had something to do with the way Daddy Scott would sometimes stop working and look beyond him, face clouded, with what might have been unborn dreams." Whatever dreams of his own life had made him cast by the wayside, he wouldn't be a roadblock standing in the way of his son's.

Shortly before his graduation from high school, Tommy turned down his father's offer of $500, a fortune for a Georgia cotton farmer to save in 1934, intended as tuition to an art school in Atlanta. A few weeks later, the medicine show came to town and Tommy got what seemed to him his chance.

He entered the medicine show's singing contest and won, and the medicine show owner, "Doc" M.F. Chamberlain, offered him a job. He had played and sung for money, he had performed on radio, and he had come to know and love "the headiness of applause." He wanted this chance. The medicine show moved on from Toccoa, southward toward Elbert County, and the young Tommy decided he would move with it. The decision brought with it to the seventeen-year-old the hardest morning of his young life.

He left before dawn and in a rainy, slipping out of the house, carrying his guitar and a cardboard suitcase. "I could not bear to go through the goodbyes again, as the last night home had been difficult enough," he recalled.

It was hardest on his little sister, Cleo, and it would be years before he knew she had gotten up to watch him go, sobbing as she watched him fade away in the dreary darkness.

He paused to look at the whitewashed house that had been his only home and at the cotton stalks sprouting from the red clay farm his father loved and thought of everything and everyone he was walking away from.

He had left with Cleo a note for Mary Frank "Frankie" Thomas, the girl who he already knew owned his heart and always would. The note said simply, "Someday …"

When he missed the bus Tommy set out to walk the roughly thirty-five miles to Elberton in the drizzle, trudging on until the driver of a truckload of chickens gave him a lift to just outside of Elberton.

He walked the rest of the way, wet, smelling of chickens and their manure, his feet chafing to bloody blisters in his wet shoes. For most of the way he wished he had stayed home, but he found the medicine show's camp around the two trucks, sides streaked with the red dirt and mud of many a country road, that carried all the shows' paraphernalia.

Chamberlain remembered the job offer made in Toccoa and followed it up with the promise to pay Tommy six dollars a week and his board. He had tried to hire a lot of guitar players, Chamberlain told him, but Tommy was the only one ever to take him up on it.

M.F. Chamberlain, an Englishman of evident education and some refinement, had begun his medicine show in 1890, traveling to wherever a crowd could be expected, even some public hangings in the early days. But the offer of novel entertainment could draw a crowd under almost any conditions, all medicine show operators found, and from that sprouted talent shows, beauty contests and traveling stage acts. The more entertainment, the bigger the crowds.

"The medicine shows were really the beginning for (talent shows and beauty contests)," Scott said. "They were the beginning of the country music industry. People who wanted to play music got the chance to earn a little money, enough that you could live on it."

Whatever it took to draw a crowd, the idea was for the people to hear along with the music the pitches for Chamberlain's Snake Oil liniment and Herb-O-Lac, an herbal laxative. Both of these Chamberlain brewed himself from recipes he claimed he'd gotten from the Cherokee.

A typical show lasted about an hour and a half, but for about forty-five minutes of that Chamberlain would preach the virtues of his potions. "He could charm the skin off a snake's backside," Scott recalled.

The young Tommy played his music but also watched and learned. Being a showman was about more that just performing on a stage. It was about winning over and holding the audience, and about building up their expectation and fulfilling them and then some. All this Chamberlain early on set out to teach him about show business.

"He treated me like a son," Scott said. "I felt he saw in me a continuation of his life's work, somebody who would carry on the herbal and entertainment show long after he was dead and gone." By the time Scott joined the show, Chamberlain had himself and a husband and wife team, who performed various acts of what Scott termed "rube comedy," involving playing exaggerated backwoods country characters. Scott himself conjured up a character called "Horsefly" and another, done in blackface, called "Peanut".

Several characters were done in blackface, something which the older Scott does not regret even in the face of twenty-first century sensitivities. "The black faces and rube characters were accepted as a part of our act in the North and South, and by all races of people," he recalled. It was a time of innocence, according to Scott, "when we did not wholly understand that our actions might have been labeled cruel. … I was a black face comedian and I make no apologies for it. I can only apologize for not knowing and for innocence."

Chamberlain also taught young Tommy one of his own skills, ventriloquism, and urged him to make his own dummy. The result was "Luke McLuke," one of Scott's most enduring creations from his long working life, whose head he carved from a piece of cypress. "When I look back," Scott said, standing amid the museum room of his house, looking at early photos of him and the dummy, "it always goes back to me and the guitar and the doll."

About two years after Tommy joined his traveling show, Chamberlain decided to retire. Tommy packed his clothes and guitar – and Luke McLuke – to head for home. At their last parting, Chamberlain drove him to the bus station and bought his ticket to Toccoa. "The last thing ol' Doc said to me," Scott recalled, "was, 'I want you to carry on the business. I have written down the formulas for the medicines for you. It is yours. I think you will make a great show man.'"

A great showman Tommy had every reason to think he would be, but at the time there seemed no ready prospect for him to carry on a medicine show. At their parting Chamberlain had tears in his eyes for the first time since Scott had known the old man.

Scott walked the last eight miles of dirt road from Toccoa to Eastanollee in another rainstorm, just as he had left that morning he had headed for Elberton. He had traveled a complete circle. He didn't have much money but he had Chamberlain's formulas. If a medicine show was what fate had in store for him, it would have to wait.

**Radio Days**

Raleigh, North Carolina, still showed clear signs the Great Depression was in town when Scott arrived there by bus some weeks after his return to Eastanollee. Many store buildings stood empty, and looked as if they had for years.

But what caught the young Tommy's eye the most were the men who stood on some street corners with guitars, playing for whatever coins passersby would give. He knew he was lucky to have the job he had come to town for.

WRAL in Raleigh was setting out to be one of the major regional stations in those days and Tommy Scott, not quite twenty years old, was joining the station's lineup. He would be working both on his own and with "Uncle Pete and Minervy," as performer John Ray and his wife billed themselves. They did comedy skits, not unlike some of those done on the medicine show stage, Scott recalled, but also fifteen-minute radio segments that resembled soap operas. Scott played his guitar and sang. Sometimes he did an act with "Luke McLuke".

As radio performers did in those days, the Rays and Scott also performed in the community, with the Rays doing their comedy and melodrama routines on stage while Scott performed during set and costume changes.

He missed his family and Frankie mightily, Scott recollected, but it was a time he remembered fondly. He had served an apprenticeship of sorts with Chamberlain's medicine show and this was a time for experimenting and refining his talent and acts, mastering his craft, building on Chamberlain's lessons. He developed his stage persona of "Texas Slim," picked up the nickname "Rambling Scotty" and formed early friendships that carried him through the years.

One was with early Western movie hero Roy Rogers, whom he met when Rogers was a guest on Scott's radio show while in Raleigh on a promotion tour for his first big movie playing himself, "Under Western Skies." The Monroe brothers from Kentucky, Bill and Charlie, were two other friends from the Raleigh years. Charlie Monroe, in fact, had been one the first people he met after stepping off the bus in Raleigh, and he had directed Tommy to a good boarding house that only charged three dollars a week for a room and meals. Bill Monroe, of course, would in time be dubbed "The Father of Bluegrass". "By the time I met them, Bill and Charlie were no longer speaking to each other," Scott recalled. "It was funny yet sort of sad in a way to see them perform without so much as a polite word between them."

Scott was also, whenever he could, writing his own songs. It would become a lifelong habit.

When the Monroe brothers broke up their act in 1939, Charlie Monroe took an offer in Wheeling, West Virginia, and asked Tommy to go with him and be part of his new band, The Kentucky Partners. The band would operate out of Wheeling's station WWVA, which blasted out with 50,000 watts, the same broadcasting power with which WSM in Nashville sent the Grand Ole Opry to several million listeners. It didn't take Tommy long to say yes.

Charlie Monroe could be a difficult man to work for, even for his friends. He wasn't generous with pay and, when on the road for out-of-station play dates, wouldn't allow his band to stay at the same hotel as he, taking his image as a radio star very seriously.

For the most part, the band slept and ate on the road, always having to be back for scheduled performances on the station, highlighted by the every Saturday night Wheeling Jamboree. But like the days in Raleigh, it was a time Tommy looked back on in later years with surpassing fondness. "Our eating habits were terrible," he recalled, "Most of the time usually consisting of stopping at some little gas station or country store for cheese, crackers and bologna, with a grape or orange pop to wash it down with." Still, when he wrote his memoirs, thoughts of the time prompted Scott to sum them up with "Those, my friend, were the days!"

They were also the days when the success of bands playing for radio stations depended on their getting sponsors who paid to have the band hawk the sponsor's products between songs and skits. And Charlie Monroe's band began running into problems finding enough sponsors. Over the time Tommy worked with him, Monroe would move his band from Wheeling to WHAS in Louisville, Kentucky, then on to WFBC in Greenville, South Carolina, and concurrently WBIG in Greensboro, North Carolina. "Bill (Monroe) was doing fine, but sponsors didn't see Charlie as an asset by himself," Tommy recalled.

Patent medicines and herbal remedies were common sponsors for radio programs and therein lay an idea: After all, Tommy had "Doc" Chamberlain's recipes.

Monroe proposed supplying the money to make Herb-O-Lac, which was renamed Manoree, and Tommy would develop distribution through drug stores and general stores. Manoree would become the new sponsors of The Kentucky Partners and any profits would be split evenly. An Ohio laboratory concocted the potion and shipped it in bulk to a Greensboro, North Carolina, drugstore for bottling.

The Manoree network soon included fifteen radio stations that carried The Kentucky Partners' show "brought to you by Manoree, the makers of the tonic laxative that keeps everybody hale, hearty and healthy." At the peak, about 10,000 bottles of the potion a week were being sold for one dollar apiece.

Before long, however, it became clear to Tommy that Monroe had no intention of dividing the Manoree profits with him, and he decided to call it quits with Charlie Monroe's band. There was one big dividend from it all, though: Tommy was, in a manner of speaking, back in the medicine show business. He would never really ever be out of it again.

By this time he and Frankie were married and were expecting a child, their only child, Sandra. His long ago promise of "someday" had come true when he and Frankie married on June 23, 1940. Frankie had also left the Eastanollee area and had been modeling clothes and jewelry in Atlanta when Tommy, mindful of the world war apparently in the winds, asked her to set a date.

Tommy was playing now at WAIM in Anderson, South Carolina, where he had first played on big time radio as a sixteen-year-old. Now joined by a good friend from the Charlie Monroe days, Curly Seckler, they were sponsored by another locally made herbal remedy, Vim Herb. They soon began a tent show, "Ramblin' Scotty and Smilin' Bill," based out of WAIM and stations in Augusta, Georgia, Spartanburg, South Carolina, and Toccoa. In time, Tommy's sister, Cleo, joined the show and would continue with Tommy until she married. Frankie Scott also became a key part of the comedy show, carrying on the role of "Clarabelle," a "little naïve mountain girl from Flintsville," in Tommy's description of her, likening the character to Grand Ole Opry star Sarah Cannon's character "Minnie Pearl". The cast would grow to include others.

When WRLC radio began in Toccoa, owner R.G. LeTourneau offered Tommy a job. He and Frankie moved from Anderson to Toccoa but he continued to work for WAIM as well. Frankie in time became a host and an operator at the Toccoa station. Meanwhile, the world war had become a reality. Tommy was ineligible for military service due to some early injuries but he supported the war effort in the only way he could.

"We did a lot of free concerts for the soldiers," he recalled. Many of those shows were for the paratroopers training at Camp Toccoa, just outside of town. His service of a sort was remembered. When "Band of Brothers," an HBO miniseries based on the wartime exploits of Easy Company of the 506th Parachute Infantry Regiment, which trained at the camp, premiered in Toccoa in 2001, Tommy and Frankie were honored guests.

In 1942, Tommy Scott abandoned the Vim Herb sponsor began once again marketing and selling Herb-O-Lac, this time under "Doc" Chamberlain's original name for the concoction.

"I had had one goal that was with me from the time 'Doc' Chamberlain put me on that bus," Tommy recalled. "I wanted to get my own medicine company up and running." But it was also evident to him that there was no real future on the road from town to town "selling a bottle here and a bottle there" at a dollar a bottle.

The small traveling troupe that by now was "Ramblin' Tommy Scott's Big Radio Show" was on the way to becoming the medicine show he dreamed of, and Tommy was laying the groundwork for an Herb-O-Lac empire.

"It cost me 33 cents to make a bottle of Herb-O-Lac," Tommy recalled. "I sold it to the stores for 66 cents and they charged a dollar."

He would consign a batch of the tonic to stores and then plug the locations along with the tonic on his radio show. Deals with stations in, at first, Gainesville and Athens in Georgia, Greenville, South Carolina, and Gastonia, North Carolina, created a small network of stations that carried his show over a telephone line as it was performed live. Before long, according to Scott, an average of one hundred requests for the potion were arriving in the mail every day besides what was being sold in stores.

Then came the day in late 1943 when Tommy Scott got a call from the Grand Ole Opry.

To most performers it would have seemed the opportunity they had dreamed of, but it was one Tommy actually had to think over. The Grand Ole Opry show was performed live over Nashville's WSM every Saturday night, which was also the biggest night for his own show. And, too, in those days the Opry didn't pay performers. The prestige and exposure was thought enough. Nevertheless, he auditioned. His singing didn't seem to overly impress the Opry's legendary impresario, "Judge" George D. Hay – "We have a lot of singers around here. We need something different," Tommy recalls Hay saying. He would have to take another tack

Tommy resurrected his act with Luke McLuke. He and his cypress-headed creation were a hit, and he was booked for the early show of the next week.

Scott was on the Grand Ole Opry every Saturday night for a year after that beginning, making more lifelong friends such as country music legends as Roy Acuff, Ernest Tubb and Minnie Pearl. But as he had reckoned and feared, performing on the Opry often stretched him to the limit.

"Wherever we were on the road, we'd have to leave where we were, go to Nashville, do a show and go back to our next stop on the road," Tommy said, wistfully. "After a while they paid you six dollars a show, but it was worth a lot more than that just to be on the Grand Ole Opry."

**Medicine Show Man**

The late 1940s were good to Tommy Scott. He had built on his earlier successes, learned from some of his early failures and was knocking on the door of his greatest popularity to come. More radio stations carried his show, through live feeds or recorded transcriptions. Herb-O-Lac became more of a household word. And record contracts, to which Tommy was already no stranger, came more often. Then, in 1948, he got an offer to make history with a new medium, television.

The chance came when the wife of a Dallas, Texas, film producer saw one of his shows during his troupe's swing through Texas theaters. There were twenty-seven television stations on the air in 1948, with an estimated 350,000 Americans owning a set. The producer saw the potential and was looking for a way to make his own mark in the emerging industry. The result was The Ramblin' Tommy Scott Show, the first country television show in history broadcasting, in Scott's preferred term, "hillbilly music".

Each show was about thirteen and a half minutes long, so that local stations could insert a minute and a half of commercials for running in whatever time slot the station scheduled. Filmed on small sets – a Western living room scene, a barn set and a radio disc jockey's booth – the shows were made of independent segments that could be mixed and matched according to time and theme. The living room scene, for instance, was designed to put viewers at ease, to create the impression that Scott was singing just for them.

"I wore a plaid shirt and sang largely to Frankie, who wore a pretty dress with a small square pattern," Scott recollected in his memoirs. "Baby Sandra would sit on the floor patting a kitten as everyone sang and played. I'd sing songs to Frankie like my 'You are the Rainbow of My Dreams,' or perhaps to Sandra "Little Baby Girl'."

The producer also marketed individual three-minute segments to movie theaters. Scott recalled that the first run of shows in 1948 was thirteen episodes, for which he got $500. But the success of the shows meant that when he returned in 1949 to film more, he got $600 – per episode.

The opportunity for short films followed, such as "Hillbilly Jamboree," "Southern Hayride," and "Hobos and Indians." But through it all, he was still, at heart, the medicine show man. The medicine and the medicine show, after all, lay at the heart of his success.

"It was the success of the medicine that allowed me to build a good stage show, pay my performers a good wage for that day and keep building so I could increase my performance area," he recalled.

The medicine show continued to roll, moving across the United States and Canada in a caravan of trucks and motor homes, with Frankie a key part of the business, and others who became Scott's performing family, such as Tim McCoy, Lash Larue and Al "Fuzzy" St. John and Gaines Blevin. Some came and went over the years, but all remained part of Scott's extended family and were never far away. In time, Sandra Scott joined in the show, performing circus acts. Later, after she married, she took over part of the business management side of the operation. The show had several names over the years, such as the Hollywood Hillybilly Jamboree and The Georgia Peanut Band, before becoming "Doc" Tommy Scott's Last Real Old Time Medicine Show, the only fulltime medicine show in the world that actually sold a patent medicine.

Scott grew wistful reflecting on the shows and the years as they piled up, his stories coming between longer and longer pauses, but the glint of humor never left his eyes as he talked about them.

Did each town stick out in his mind after the years? No, not really.

"All places are just about the same," he said. "And some small towns just got monotonous. What you recall is the time that a door wouldn't open when it was supposed to, or when you got locked in a room, but you don't always remember where it was.

"Or sometimes you'd forget from show to show in a place what you had done in the last show," Scott said. "I'd wonder 'Did I tell this joke last night or earlier in this show?' Sometimes I'd go ahead and tell it and the people would say 'You done told that!'

"But I've got ways of getting around that," he said, laughing. "That's just showmanship."

The traveling medicine show slowed and gradually came to an end when Frankie Scott fell ill. She was as much a part of the show as she was of Tommy Scott's life. He lost her in 2004, to Alzheimer's Syndrome. As Tommy put it, "Frankie left me little by little. But some of her last complete sentences were 'I have a good husband' and 'I love you'. ...I had a wonderful lifetime with that precious woman."

Tommy Scott died on September 30, 2013, some months after the interview in his home that provided much of the grist for this story. He was ninety-six, and his death was the result of injuries suffered in a car accident over a month before. He was a man of great warmth and humor. On meeting him for the first time, you felt you had met a longtime friend, and it's not hard to imagine that quality to be what came through to almost countless audiences for over eight decades and was the foundation for his worldwide acclaim.

Tommy Scott wrote what could serve as his best epitaph in his memoirs published in 2007, when writing about how he loved performing for an audience:

"I have often said that when my time is up on this earth, I hope the big Medicine Man in the sky will push a button and allow me to hear all the applause again ... heaven!"

*Based on an interview with Tommy Scott at his home, with recollections used by his permission from his autobiography "Snake Oil, Superstars and Me," by Scott, Shirley Noe and Randall Franks.*

# 5

# Death Comes to "the meanest man in Georgia"

Just after four in the afternoon on November 17, 1900, in the small, dozy Elbert County hamlet of Heardmont. William Mattox and his son-in-law, Jeptha Jones, stalked toward each other with their revolvers blasting. Not more than twenty minutes later, the sixty-four-year-old Mattox was dead.

The duel had begun over a horse. At least that was the tale as it was told, the story attested to by the witnesses at the inquest. But there was more to the story. Jones was later reported to have told his wife that in shooting her father he "had done what he wanted to do."

A lot of people had probably felt that way about William Mattox in his life, especially if he held some position of power over them. He had, after all, been widely labeled "the meanest man in Georgia," the subject of black minstrel ditties alluding to his brutality toward the leased convicts who had worked his cotton farms along the upper Savannah River after the Civil War.

He had been born of rough-hewn pioneer stock on a farm in the North Georgia back country of the upper Savannah River Valley. But antebellum family prosperity had brought him the opportunity to become a classically educated man, a man who by accounts could combine his erudition with considerable native charm and eloquence, all qualities he would in time parlay all the way to the Georgia legislature.

That was one side of the man. The other side was a brutal and savage side to the man, one especially well known to those he stood over or who stood in his way.

Of that there is evidence aplenty.

He was a scion of the Old South, a one time Confederate Army officer, but he had also been among the first to grasp the essence of celebrated *Atlanta Constitution* editor Henry Grady's New South, and was set on attempting to lead his own quiet corner of the world toward Grady's vision of factories side by side with farms. William Faulkner, wading into the swamps and scrub pine woods of his fictional Yoknapatawpha County, Mississippi, could not have plucked from them a character more telling in the qualities, good and bad, of the class of leaders who rose from the ashes of the Old South to forge a new order.

Nor could Faulkner have imagined a better end for him as Mattox's worst qualities won out. By 1900, his new business ventures had failed, taking away most of his once large fortune and much of his status. And finally Mattox's infamous temper and violent streak led his son-in-law to lay him low in the middle of a dusty Heardmont road.

William Henry Mattox, was born January 5, 1836, in Elbert County, the son of Henry Page Mattox, planter and onetime state legislator. The Mattox family had migrated to Georgia from central Virginia in the mid-1780s. They were of a group of Virginians led south by George Mathews, future Georgia governor and Yazoo Land Fraud figure, a group that also included a youngster named Meriwether Lewis whose widowed mother had married a Mathews crony, John Marks. The Mattox clan settled first with the rest of Mathews's party in what became the Goose Pond area of Wilkes and Oglethorpe counties, along the Broad River.[1]

The family prospered. By 1842, Henry Mattox, then thirty-one and living in Elbert County, was able to pay $5,000 for 673 acres along the Elbert County side of the Broad River. Here, too, the Mattox family thrived. The Mattox holdings increased and in 1852 young William was sent to Franklin College (the University of Georgia after 1859).

He made the best of it, despite having no apparent scholarly ambitions. In later years he would make a great impression on others with the depth and breadth of his classical education.[2]

Graduating in 1856, he immediately started laying the foundation of what would become his own empire. Probably with his father's backing, he began acquiring land in Elbert County along the Savannah River near the mouth of Beaverdam Creek. In 1858, he bought three hundred acres around Cherokee Ford on the Savannah and the next year added another nearby 732 acres to his holdings. Along the way he also acquired seventy-nine slaves.[3]

He also made the time-honored good move of marrying well. In 1858 he married Rebecca Allen, a daughter of Singleton Allen. Singleton's father, William, had established a prosperous plantation and mercantile business along Beaverdam Creek in the 1790s, coupled with some business interests in the thriving river port of Petersburg at the confluence of the Broad and Savannah Rivers. The only blemish on the Allen name came from William's brother Beverly, a defrocked Methodist minister who had shot and killed U.S. marshal Robert Forsyth in a dispute in 1794. With the help of friends, William had freed Beverly from jail, enabling him to escape to Kentucky, where he lived out his remaining years. With the passing of years, however, that episode had actually burnished the Allen name in Elbert County, Beverly Allen's exploits having become the stuff of local legend. Singleton Allen had married the daughter of a prosperous local planter, Georgia's one time provisional governor Stephen Heard, and by the time the young up and coming planter William Mattox married into the family the Allens were part of the local landed gentry.

Mattox's buying of land adjoining rapidly flowing rivers and streams hints that he might have been looking to build mills even at this time, but as with so many others the coming of the war meant he had to postpone his plans. As events unfolded, however, he would be less inconvenienced and hindered by the war than most others.

In the summer of 1861, he was elected a second lieutenant in the McIntosh Volunteers, a company formed by his brother-in-law, William McPherson McIntosh, and kept the rank when the company became Company I of the 15th Georgia Infantry. The regiment would be among those forces in gray who missed the Battle of First Manasass in July 1861,, but Virginia was their destination. On Christmas Day, 1861, he was promoted to captain.

Despite his promotion, however, soldiering did not seem to agree with him (or he did not agree with soldiering). As early as the previous September he had fallen ill. "Bill Mattox has not held up as well as I have," McIntosh, by then the 15th Georgia's commander, wrote another brother-in-law, Young L. G. Harris, on Sept. 26, 1861. "He is even now under the weather, not confined to his bed but complaining. I got him into a house not far from camp, where he is doing well, and I hope will soon be able to return to duty."[4]

The 15th Georgia was stationed in northern Virginia, in the vicinity of the Manassas battlefield, for a good deal of the winter of 1861-62 and was involved in occasional skirmishing. There is no record, however, of Mattox being involved in any fighting or even being in the field with the regiment during this time instead of laid up with apparent illness.

In any case, on April 9, 1862, he resigned his commission. By this time McIntosh had been promoted to colonel commanding the regiment, in the brigade of his friend and sometimes law practice associate, Robert A. Toombs of Washington, Georgia, former U.S. congressman, former U.S. senator, former Confederate secretary of state, now a brigadier general. On June 27, 1862, McIntosh would be mortally wounded leading the 15th Georgia into an attack at the Battle of Garnett's Farm.

By that time Mattox had been home in Georgia for nearly three months. In that alone, though, he was hardly unique. The spring of 1862 had seen many officers resign as conditions or regimental politics caused soldiering to lose its luster. Ironically, to the end of his days Mattox would be known as "Colonel Mattox" in the way that more than a few men who rose to postwar prominence were endowed with an honorary title they hadn't earned. His desultory record in uniform, however, did not prevent him from trading on his Confederate Army service in his postwar political ballyhooing.

Accounts of Mattox's activities on the home front as the war marched on are sketchy, except for his recorded new acquisitions of property. But stories suggest that he was looking to come out of the war a prosperous man in the midst of hard times all around. He succeeded.

To do it, he exploited the shortage and dearness of hard money in the South at the same time depreciating Confederate money became more worthless by the day. During the war he borrowed $10,000 in gold specie from Mildred "Miss Millie" Gray, a local lady of some wealth who was related to Mattox by marriage.

Hard money was in short supply in substantial amounts in the South even before the war, but a circumstance had placed this trove in Mildred Gray's possession (and Mattox's reach). She had inherited considerable property and money from her deceased first husband, Beverly Allen, son of William Allen and brother of Mattox's father-in-law, Singleton Allen (and nephew of the original, notorious Beverly). By family accounts, the brothers Singleton and Beverly Allen had ventured into the North Georgia gold fields around Dahlonega and Auraria and increased the family fortunes. The accounts seem well founded. An elderly descendant of Mildred Gray has recounted that as a boy in the 1930s he played over old gold mining machinery the brothers had brought back and stored in a barn. The borrowed money might even have been in coins minted at the Dahlonega mint, but that is solely speculation.

Whatever the coinage, however, the loan wasn't repaid in kind. Mattox did repay the loan before the end of the war – but he repaid it in Confederate currency. As late as the 1930s, descendants of the Gray family retained the stacks and bundles of Confederate money Mattox had given in repayment.[5]

At a time when others faced the hardship of the war on the home front, Mattox was spending money, investing in both land and in mills. By early in 1865 he, along with some partners, had acquired Eureka Mill on upper Beaverdam Creek, for $4,854. The core of this grist mill operation dated from about 1820 and had been expanded several times over the years under different owners. By the time Mattox bought into it, it was owned by the Rucker family, having been acquired by Joseph Rucker, a local planter and banker reputed to have been Georgia's first millionaire.

Mattox was also laying the groundwork for an even larger mill on his property at Cherokee Ford on the Savannah River.

This new mill would be the crown jewel of Mattox's milling operations until he decided, in 1889, to venture into textile milling. Built just below the actual ford, one of the major crossing points on the upper river since colonial times, the mill had a mill race of about a mile, running from a diversion dam that stretched from the Georgia bank to McCalla's Island, lying about midway the river and delivering a drop of sixteen feet at the mill. The water powered five turbines at the mill's zenith of operations in the 1880s, turning two sets of mill stones that could turn an estimated two hundred bushels of grain a day into flour or meal. For the time and place, it was a large mill in size and capacity.[6]

It was only a part of Mattox's empire, however. By the mid-1880s, his land holdings totaled 3,414 acres, mostly rich bottom lands stretching along the Georgia side of the upper Savannah River and including two islands in the river itself. Records show he employed forty people to operate his mills and farms, but that doesn't tell the whole story.

The ending of slavery had barely slowed Mattox's farming operations. The postwar Federal Army occupation government had put in place a system of leasing state prisoners. These convicts leased from the state provided a cheap source of labor, especially for owners of large farms, little different in practice from slavery, only without the capital investment.

By the 1880s, Mattox had a well-established convict stockade on his upper Savannah River lands, near his milling operation and on the Georgia side across from Carter's Island, one of his river island holdings. Mattox seemed to favor leasing black women, presumably because they were less likely to attempt escape than men.

In time he acquired a reputation for cruelty in his treatment of his leased convicts. Unlike the times before the war, after all, with leased convicts there was no incentive to look very much to the well-being of the workers. If one died, for whatever reason, the state would send another to take the dead convict's place. A man who was one of Mattox's stockade guards in his youth, "Bud" Hilley, recounted in the 1930s tales of Mattox's brutality that can still chill the blood.

Early every morning, according to Hilley, the convicts were moved across to the island farms. In one story, vividly related, a convict did not show up one morning at the ferry landing. When found in the bunkhouse that sheltered the convicts she claimed illness; nevertheless, she went to the boat. Mattox himself was there on that occasion and, learning the reason for the delay in starting the workday, he beat and kicked her until she was a bloody mess. Occasionally, in Hilley's telling, a child would be born to one of the convicts. No time could be spared for a nursing mother, so on Mattox's standing orders the newborn was simply taken to the river and thrown in.[7]

Mattox's reputation for cruelty spread far and wide. It even found its way into a black minstrel ditty that made the rounds:

>    Beef steak when I'se hungry
>
>    Likker when I'se dry
>
>    Greenbacks when I'se hard up
>
>    And 'ligion when I die
>
>
>    Bill Mattox is yo master
>
>    Bill Mattox is yo frin
>
>    Bill Mattox totes de long cowhide
>
>    He ain't afraid to bend!
>
>
>    Miss Beck 'vite yo' in de parlor
>
>    Dey fan ya' wid' de fan
>
>    Oh mudder, oh dear mudder
>
>    I luvs dat gamblin' man

The words seem harmless enough, but the hint implied in the mentioned "long cowhide" is that they conceal a lot of irony, typical of some minstrel lyrics. John M. McIntosh, who published a history of Elbert County in 1940, recounted that some time during his years of prominence Mattox was walking down Broad Street in Augusta when he heard a black man singing this ditty. When he inquired about it, Mattox was asked, in effect, "Why haven't you ever heard of ol' Bill Mattox? He's the meanest man in Georgia."

A chase down the street ensued, according to accounts, with the singer narrowly staying ahead of Mattox's swinging cane. McIntosh wrote that Mattox in later years would tell the tale himself, in good humor.[8] An anecdotal profile of Mattox that appeared in the July 23, 1889 edition of the *Elberton Star*, however, noted that the reporter had managed to coax an old man employed in the Mattox home to play the ditty on a banjo only after he was assured Mattox was nowhere around, the playing being forbidden when Mattox was in the house.[9]

Mattox also made a play at increasing his political fortunes. He was elected as a representative to the state legislature in 1865. He was later elected to the state senate for a term in 1880-81. In between, he was elected as a delegate to the 1877 constitutional convention, which fashioned a post-Reconstruction state government. His biography in the official record of the convention describes him as "a gentleman of large culture and refinement, a forcible and pleasant speaker, and exceedingly popular." It's difficult to say whether this accurately reflected the view of Mattox around Atlanta. Even the worse sorts, after all, are likely to be praised by friends and enemies alike in official biographies. But whatever the truth, Mattox never gained a reputation as a widely powerful political figure. At least not publicly, though it's easy to see him as a likely political gamesman of the smoke-filled rooms. If anything, he might have even preferred it that way.[10]

By 1889, Mattox was ready to make the big leap from owning grist mills to building textile mills. That was the theme of a new age for the South. It was only three years after Henry Grady, editor of the *Atlanta Constitution*, had delivered his famous speech to the New England Society of New York at New York City's famous Delmonico's restaurant, to a group that included among others the famous financier and Wall Street impresario J.P. Morgan. Grady had pronounced the Old South dead. The old way of life, he said, "rested everything on slavery and agriculture, unconscious that these could neither give nor maintain healthy growth." The New South, he opined, would embody many new ideas, including "a diversified industry that meets the complex needs of this complex age." On July 23, 1889, Grady visited Elberton, a carnival-like visit to promote his progressive thinking arranged by a committee chaired by Mattox and ballyhooed by the local newspaper echoing the support of all the local boosters. Mattox pronounced Grady's speech as "the best and most forward thinking I've ever heard." That day's edition of the *Elberton Star* also carried the announcement of the intention of Mattox and a group of partners to bring more of the New South to Elbert County.[11]

Mattox and a group of investors that included his son-in-law, Jeptha Jones Jr., his son-in-law's father, Jeptha Jones, Sr. and a brother-in-law, John McCalla, purchased a mill site and water rights on Beaverdam Creek. They purchased it, ironically, from the nephew and heir of Mildred Gray, Mattox's lender during the war. Like the gold specie, Mildred Gray had inherited the mill by way of the Allen family.

The creek along that stretch had a good fall and a steady bold flow. Though the Allens didn't build the first grist mill there, they had expanded the original mill, dating back to 1811, into a substantial enterprise. Now, Mattox and his partners intended, it would be the site of the county's first large scale cotton mill. The Heardmont Cotton Mill was incorporated in the fall of 1889, with Mattox, the principal investor, as president and McCalla as secretary-treasurer. The New South, or at least William Mattox's version of it, would rise on the banks of Beaverdam Creek.

To raise his share of the start up capital, Mattox was willing to make a sizable wager – the lion's share of his holdings. In 1889, he mortgaged the gristmill and the associated land near Cherokee Ford as well as much of his other land. Mattox himself made a trip to New England to purchase the new mill's machinery. When the mill opened in March 1890, a new water turbine system provided power to eight cording machines and frames holding 1,000 spindles, producing cotton yarding from lint cotton that was a by-product of the already existing

Elberton Oil Mill. Mattox stated to the local newspaper that the venture was an experiment; if it succeeded and proved profitable the partners planned to expand it into one of the largest mills in the South.[12]

That was not to be. On June 16, however, barely three months after it began production, the Heardmont Cotton Mill was struck by lightning during a thunderstorm. The resulting fire destroyed the mill, and with it the hopes of the would-be textile barons. There was no fire insurance; the loss was entirely the owners' to bear. The mill site would sit idle until 1895, when Thomas Swift, owner of the Swift Cotton Mill in Elberton, purchased the tract and built Pearle Mill, named for his daughter.

William Mattox could only watch from afar as another man's dreams rose from the ashes of his own. He had bet and lost, and the destruction of the Heardmont Cotton Mill was the beginning of the end for him. The loss of his investment, backed by his mortgaged property, triggered a cascade of financial ruin. He was unfortunate that his and his partners' personal calamity coincided with one of the major downturns in the American economy, part of a worldwide economic crisis. It all added up to being a bad time to try to stance the bleeding of financial wounds.

A fall off in new building and railroad investment, continued debate over bimetallism and whether gold or silver values would determine money supply, contractions of credit, industrial production and consumption pressures in Europe–all these added up to a depression by 1893, one of the worst in world and American history.

Unemployment in the industrial sections of the country climbed to an estimated 18 percent in 1894 and stayed in the 12-14 percent range until 1898. In the South, where 60 percent of the labor force was agricultural and many farms were mortgaged, prices of commodities plummeted: Cotton, which had averaged over 15 cents per pound since the 1870s, dropped to just over 7 cents, especially since much of the foreign market was lost to the new emerging markets of Egypt and India. Bad judgment or bad luck and bad timing, it's difficult to say what caused Mattox's slide downward. But his fall would be even more speedy than his rise. A karmic view might hold that in some mystical

Ledger of Life he was fated to balance some account by losing all he'd gained on a mill site bought from the estate of a woman he had virtually flimflammed out of $10,000 in gold. By 1898, he was bankrupt. That year the Equitable Insurance Company, a New York City investment bank, sued him for his debts and most of his property was sold at public auction in Elberton for $16,000. The New York company itself bought most of the property.[13]

As one of the investors in the Heardmont Cotton Mill, Jeptha Jones Jr's father had also suffered a financial calamity. Jeptha Jr. had suffered as well, but as only a minor investor he was spared the near total catastrophe that engulfed his father and father-in-law. Bad blood developed between Mattox and the Joneses that grew more poisoned as time went on, even more so, evidently, between Mattox and his son-in-law.

The trigger that spilled the blood was a horse, a fine gray horse Mattox had given his daughter. Now, though, for whatever reason, need or simple spite for Jones, Mattox wanted it back. When William Mattox boarded a train in Elberton on that Saturday afternoon of Nov. 17, 1900, heading for Heardmont to confront Jones, he evidently intended to have either the horse or a widowed daughter. What Jones might have known or suspected beforehand is unclear; he left no written or spoken account. But he was already near the station and armed with at least two guns when Mattox alighted at the Heardmont depot.

Heardmont was a collection of stores and houses crowded around the depot, the last train stop before the trestle across the Savannah River into South Carolina. The little village in the red dirt cotton country of Elbert County actually preceded the coming of the railroad, though, and had sprung up at a nexus of a web of roads as the center of a thriving farming community, complete with stores and a school. The land the community sat on, as well as most surrounding it, had once belonged to Stephen Heard. The former governor in fact lay in his family cemetery on a hill overlooking the depot. William M. McIntosh, Mattox's brother-in-law and former regimental commander, lay at rest there, too, in 1900 dead thirty-eight years since his being cut down by a Yankee bullet. The little community remained a stronghold of various branches of the Heard and Allen families, which of course included William Mattox and Jeptha Jones. Mattox's main convict stockade had sat a short distance from the depot, but Georgia's leasing of convicts had ended earlier that year.

**The Showdown**

Mattox got off the train from Elberton shortly after 4 p.m., according to the later inquest testimony of M. D. Alexander, who at the time he first saw Mattox was standing in the road beside the depot talking to a local doctor named Lovern. Mattox approached, Alexander related, and asked Dr. Lovern for the loan of a horse, and at some point asked both men if they had seen Jeptha Jones.

Jones had arrived in the vicinity of depot earlier, though how much earlier isn't clear. The newspaper account of the incident, with testimony from several onlookers, is confusing and some details have to be deduced from between the lines. Local resident George Stewart testified that he had been standing on the steps of the McCalla store when Jones had come by in a buggy, shouting to Stewart that he wanted to see him. Jones continued on to the depot, a gray horse trailing behind the buggy. Stewart doesn't mention Jones' young son Allen or Jones's brother Henry being in the buggy, though both were present at the depot during the shooting. Henry Jones later testified his brother had been at the cotton gin, some distance from the depot, when the passenger train from Elberton arrived and left. Stewart followed Jones's beckoning to the depot, and began helping switch the gray horse for the horse in the buggy harness.

Alexander in his testimony didn't explicitly say whether he or the doctor told Mattox that Jones was near, only that Mattox started toward where Jones's buggy was parked.

Mattox approached, and ordered, Jeppie Mattox, a twelve-year-old black boy standing nearby, to take charge of the horse. If Jones had been out of Mattox's sight before – and that's unclear from accounts – he appeared now. "You've nothing to do with that horse, that's mine," Jones told Mattox. Mattox replied that if Jones wouldn't give up the horse then they would have to shoot it out.

Jones replied, "Well then, get to it", and stood with his right hand in his pocket, calmly watching his father-in-law some eight to ten feet away. Jones had a shotgun in his buggy, as was later established, but his pistol was more readily at hand. Mattox said, "I'll show you, then," and pulled his pistol and started shooting.

William Mattox fired first. All witnesses agreed on that. Mattox and Jones started toward each other, firing away. How many shots each man fired, witnesses could not agree on. Alexander thought Mattox fired twice and that Jones got off three shots as the two closed the distance between them. Jones later said he thought Mattox fired three times while he had fired five. Jones was correct. Judging from bullet holes later found in Mattox's coat, three of Jones's bullets had missed.

Two had hit Mattox, but he continued on apparently unfazed, through rage and sheer will. Mattox dropped his gun as the men reached each other. It was scooped up by Allen Jones but his uncle Henry took it away from him as both watched Mattox and Jeptha Jones grapple hand to hand and fall to the ground wrestling over Jones's gun.

Alexander and several others had run toward the sound of the gunshots. When they arrived, they saw the two men on the ground, Mattox astride a prostrate Jones, both struggling, and it seemed to Alexander that Mattox was getting the better of the fight. Henry Jones was standing nearby with a gun in his hands. Alexander thought he heard Henry Jones yelling "Give brother a fair chance" to Mattox. Others thought it was Jeptha Jones himself who was yelling for Mattox to give him a chance.

Alexander managed to wrench the gun from the two men's grasp while a man named Porter pulled Mattox off Jones and to his feet. Mattox said, "Boys, he has killed me," and started to slump. The men carried him into the depot and laid him on a table.

An examination by Dr. Lovern revealed the severity of Mattox's two bullet wounds, one near dead center of his chest and the other a bit more to the right. Mattox's heart had evidently been only narrowly missed and the other wound was through his upper right lung. The internal bleeding was fatal. Mattox died about fifteen minutes after he was carried into the depot.

Jones suffered a scratch to his head, and witnesses were divided on whether it resulted from a glancing pistol shot or from his gun barrel during the fight. He went to his home, not far away, and told his wife of the shooting. Gip Verdel, a farmworker who witnessed this exchange, later testified Jones told his wife matter-of-factly that he had shot her father, "and had done what he wanted to do."

Jones and his brother both then surrendered to the county sheriff. The inquest held on Nov. 21 cleared both men, ruling the shooting justifiable homicide.

William Mattox's body was taken to Elberton and his funeral was held the very next day. His Masonic lodge took charge of the funeral arrangements. According to the newspaper account, "The procession was the largest seen in Elberton in years, showing with what esteem the deceased was held by our people."[14]

But it was the end of the barely begun Mattox dynasty.

William Henry Mattox lies in a quiet, nearly forgotten corner of Elberton's Elmhurst Cemetery. His only grave marker is one of the kind erected by the Sons of Confederate Veterans. Compared to the monuments within sight, some those of his one-time business associates, his is practically a pauper's grave. The marker lists no dates of birth and death, only his name and that he served in Company I of the 15th Georgia Infantry.

And even the marker is wrong, giving his ending rank as a second lieutenant. Nothing remains of his empire except the stories of it, and of him.

# 6
# Murder In Milledgeville: The Rage Of Marion Stembridge

Milledgeville's Wayne Street, the late 1940s.
Marion Stembridge's store was on this street.

Saturday, May 2, 1953 was the day all Milledgeville had eagerly awaited.

Red, white and blue bunting draped the buildings of the downtown like Spanish moss. Men and women walked about in the fashions of the 1800s, many of the men wearing full beards grown as celebratory Brothers of the Brush. Some men carried makeshift muskets in which they set off firecrackers. Displays in downtown store windows ballyhooed the town's long and rich history.

Milledgeville was poised to kick off the celebration of its sesquicentennial, marking the city's founding in 1803 as Georgia's new capital. It was a celebration to be done right and done big. A parade was on tap for the afternoon for the main kick off, with a grand ball to follow that evening. That gala would see the crowning of a sesquicentennial queen, an honor much coveted by local young women.

A full slate of parties, picnics and pageants had been arranged for all the next week. One day of that week Governor Herman Talmadge was scheduled to visit. The big doings had been a year in the planning, and even the weather was cooperating for the big kickoff. The heavy rains of the past week had given way to clear skies, the big inaugural day dawning sunny and clear.[1]

At a little after 10 a.m., Marion Stembridge walked past those lined up to see the Western movie "Dead Man's Trail" at the Campus Theater on Hancock Street, the town's main thoroughfare, and started up the stairs leading to the suite of offices above the theater. The sixty-one-year-old banker and store owner appeared as he always did. He wore a neatly pressed suit and a soft felt wide-brimmed hat pulled down low. As everyone in Milledgeville had grown accustomed to seeing him, Stembridge was stone-faced, unsmiling, peering out at the world through thick glasses that distorted his eyes and gave him a look described as "cold and crazy".[2]

"Crazy" was how most of the townspeople would have described Marion Stembridge. Over the past five years his reputation had shaded from merely eccentric to almost certainly insane – if the stories circulating about his peculiar lifestyle were true. What was undeniably true was that his so-called banking business was nothing more than loansharking and that he had a mean streak as wide as a country mile. Four years before, he had been convicted of manslaughter after a shooting incident stemming from his lending but had avoided serving any time in jail. The why of that was still a mystery to Milledgevillians. And just the previous Monday Stembridge had been convicted in federal court in Macon of tax evasion and of attempting to bribe agents of the Internal Revenue Service. The account in the Milledgeville *Union-Recorder* that week had reported the details, as well as that Stembridge was to report to court the coming Monday for sentencing. Despite all that, Stembridge was always "cool on the surface" and impeccably well-mannered in public. For most people, though, he was a character best avoided.[3]

When Stembridge hurried back out into the street, one six-year-old waiting with his mother excitedly told her that the man had a gun. The boy's mother assured him the pistol in the man's hand was just a toy, like the muskets the other men were carrying. Meanwhile Stembridge hurried by and started up the steps of the Sanford Building, next door to the theater. Some of the people he passed later recalled that he tipped his hat as he went by. A few moments later, a woman shouted from a window above the theater that attorney Marion Ennis had been shot.[4]

Quickly the city police and the county sheriff and his deputies began converging on the downtown, sirens blaring. Rumors of what had happened spread like wildfire in dry grass and the streets filled with people. Local historian Louis Andrews remembered one man riding up and down Hancock Street in his car, tires squealing, horn blaring, trying to alert everyone about the shooting. "He was so excited he couldn't even talk," Andrews recalled. Streets near the scene quickly became so congested that people had to park blocks away and walk into downtown. "It was one terrible morning," said Andrews.[5]

Eugene Ellis, active and razor-sharp at eighty-nine when interviewed for this story, was the Milledgeville police chief in 1953, and for him the events of that morning are as crystal clear as any he recalls from a lifetime in law enforcement. "I got a call that there had been a shooting at the Campus Theater," said Ellis. "When I got there, the sheriff, Dennis Cox, told me that Marion Stembridge had killed Marion Ennis in his law office and had gone into the Sanford Building." The men started up the stairs. Ellis cautioned Cox that if they rushed up the stairs they would be "sitting ducks," that they had better go slow.

Halfway up the stairs, the men heard a shot. When Ellis crept near the top and peered up into the hallway leading off the stairs, he saw Stembridge lying facedown in front of the office of Judge Edwin Sibley.

Gun in hand, Ellis approached slowly. He saw a gun in Stembridge's hand and thought Stembridge might be "playing possum" despite the blood pooling around his head. He put one foot on Stembridge's wrist and kicked the gun away with the other. But Stembridge had been dead from the moment he had put the barrel of a .38 cal. revolver in his mouth and pulled the trigger, apparently after hearing Ellis and Cox approaching up the stairs and seeing no chance of escaping them. Before killing himself, Ellis and Cox soon found, he had committed a second murder, of attorney Stephen "Pete" Bivens.

As Ellis knelt over Stembridge's body, he felt a hand on his shoulder. It was the local state solicitor, Shep Baldwin. "To this day," said Ellis, "I don't know how he got there, I don't remember hearing him walk up on me, but when I looked around, he just said, 'It's over now, ain't it, boy?'"[6]

**An Infamous Legacy**

The fears and troubles of those whose lives had become entangled with Marion Stembridge's were indeed finally over. Stembridge had ended all that with his suicide, but not before also ending the lives of two of Milledgeville's most prominent citizens unlucky enough to be drawn into his twisted tale – two of many he had apparently planned to kill that morning. But the legacy of the Stembridge's life and the tragedy he brought about at its end was far from over. Stembridge's murderous spree itself became a landmark event in the town's history that nearly overshadowed memories of the town's sesquicentennial and colors memories of locals to this day. "For years, it seemed not a lot of people wanted to talk about [Stembridge's rampage]," said Bob Wilson, associate professor of history at Milledgeville's Georgia College & State University and a maven of local history. "It was a black mark on the town. ... Only in recent years have those who remember it or know much about it seemed comfortable talking about it."[7]

Some talk about it for the effect it had on them. "Everybody in Milledgeville who was around then remembers where they were and what they were doing when they heard about it," said James Jossey, retired as a captain from the Milledgeville Police Department and later chief of detectives for the Baldwin County Sheriff's Department.

Jossey, ten-years-old at the time, was in a drugstore down the street that morning looking at comic books after his weekly haircut. "I remember seein' em bring Ennis's and Biven's bodies out," he said. "They were covered in sheets, but the sheets looked like somebody had dumped a bucket of blood over'em. Those were the first murdered people I ever saw."[8]

In 1989 the memory of Stembridge's murders took on new life when writer Pete Dexter published *Paris Trout*, which he loosely based on the stories of Stembridge that he had heard growing up in Milledgeville. In 1991 *Paris Trout* became a movie starring Dennis Hopper in the title role. Many in Milledgeville didn't take kindly to the book or the movie, looking upon them, even as loosely based as they were, as the reopening of an old wound coupled with a gratuitous rubbing of salt. For his part, Dexter never claimed his book was history. "Obviously, I based *Paris Trout* on real events, but it is a novel," he explained in 1991. "No one should infer that all of it is true."[9] The exposure was jolting, however, and historian Wilson thinks the perceived distortions and exaggerations of the book and the movie may have prompted those reluctant to dwell on the incident to talk more about what had really happened.

The development of the community's sensitivity and perspective would come over years. When the wounds of the community were still fresh, in the first days and weeks that followed Stembridge's rampage, other concerns mattered the most.

How had Stembridge's murders and suicide come about, and most of all, why? The answers to those questions took them deep into the strange world of Marion Stembridge, for the first time stripped of all rumors had hearsay, and brought to light even more about his twisted life than many even suspected. And after learning the answers they had craved, many probably just wanted to forget it all.

### A Strange and Dangerous Man

Marion Wesley Stembridge was born in 1892 into a prominent and prosperous Baldwin County family. "They were nice people," said Eugene Ellis, "easy to get along with, all except for Marion." Evidently, whatever shaped Marion Stembridge into what he became started early in his life and seemed to have been apparent to some of his family. When Stembridge was nineteen, his older brother, Roger, and a sister tried to get him committed to the state hospital in Milledgeville. Marion's mother opposed the move, insisting that he was completely normal. For the rest of his life Marion hated his brother, and alienated himself from all of his family except his mother and two sisters. When eventually his mother went to live with Roger and his wife near the state hospital, where Roger headed the sanitation department, Marion would often come to visit her but refused to set foot in Roger's home. Instead, mother and son would talk through a side window. For a time, the widow Stembridge also apparently provided Marion with financial support, which he seemed to think his due. As his sister-in-law later described him, "He thought he was the crown prince of the family."[10]

Whatever quirks the younger Marion Stembridge exhibited, he was regarded as extremely intelligent, even "brilliant, bordering on genius." In time he would graduate from the University of Georgia School of Law but never applied for admission to the bar.

He entered the Army during World War I, but was discharged for medical reasons. Years after Stembridge's death, his sister-in-law revealed the belief within the family that whatever happened to him in the Army had exacerbated whatever mental problems he may have already had. In the 1930s, Stembridge actually did voluntarily spend several months in a mental institution. But he never revealed the reasons that led him to take that step, not even to his family.[11]

In the 1920s, Stembridge started a mail order business that allowed him to amass capital reputed to be about $160,000, a considerable fortune in middle Georgia for the time. He parlayed that stake into a complex and varied array of interests. In time, he acquired a mercantile and grocery store near Milledgeville's downtown, a timber, pulpwood and lumber yard on the outskirts of the city, and several houses and parcels of real estate around town and out in the county. He also started the Stembridge Banking Company, a private, unincorporated bank that he ran out of the rear of his store. This venture would come to most readily reflect to the community his darker side. As later became clear, long before May 1953, the bank was little more than a front for loansharking, making high-interest loans mainly to the poorer black community and habitually using written contracts that took advantage of the illiterate.

At the time of his death, Stembridge's fortune would be estimated at about $750,000, with well over half of that the assets of the bank. Ultimately, it would be Stembridge's dealings in this business that set in train the course of events leading to that fateful Saturday Milledgeville would never forget.[12]

Over those first years, Milledgevillians came to know several facets of Marion Stembridge. Those who dealt with him in his store or wood businesses knew a hard-nosed businessman, reserved and decidedly uncongenial but always polite, with almost courtly manners.

"Marion just didn't have any small talk for anybody," was how former State Court Judge Robert Green described him. But those who borrowed money from him knew him to be ruthless, a man both hated and feared by those in debt to him. Green, who as first a magistrate and then a young lawyer handled many routine legal matters (usually forced collections) for Stembridge during those years, recollected that much of Stembridge's banking business was "just inside the law."[13]

His obvious quirks clearly marked him as an eccentric, but perhaps harmlessly so, some thought. It was known and gossiped about, for instance, that he ate only cheese and canned foods, and that when he selected the cans he always took them from the back of the store shelves, never the front. Once he sent a case of canned food away to be analyzed for contamination, including a diagram of how the cans were to be arranged when the case was returned. When the cans were returned not in his preferred order, he refused to touch them.

He was also known to go armed. That was not especially unusual for the time and place, except that Stembridge always carried several guns. In his coat pocket he habitually carried a German Army-issue 9mm Walther P-38 semi-automatic (a bit unusual as a pocket pistol, but probably someone's war relic). And, according to Eugene Ellis, he was almost never without a briefcase that always contained at least two guns. He painted the sight blades of his guns white to compensate for his poor eyesight. Locals who judged him harmless came to a different verdict, though, during the last five turbulent years of Stembridge's life, as his private quirks became more public and his violent streak and legal troubles brought to light his darkest nature.[14]

In July 1947, Stembridge stunned most Milledgevillians by marrying Sarah Jordan Terry, a one-time English teacher at the Women's College of Georgia (later Georgia College). The new Mrs. Stembridge was described by many who knew her as "big, and mean as sin," perhaps a match for the mercurial Marion. Apparently, the marriage was far from a happy one, and when Sarah Stembridge filed for divorce in the spring of 1953 her allegations gave townspeople more of a glimpse into Marion Stembridge's odd private life and piled more troubles onto those that led to his final snap.[15]

The downfall of Marion Stembridge began in the fall of 1948, with an event that also brought him into contact with Eugene Ellis for the first time. Ellis had joined the Milledgeville Police Department in 1946, fresh out the Army, where he had served in the military police at Camp Wheeler, near Macon. He had served with and come to know many native Milledgevillians while there and had decided to stay in Georgia instead of returning to his native Maine, where he had been a deputy sheriff. He would become chief of the Milledgeville police on New Year's Day 1949.

"That day [in 1948] I got a call that there had been a shooting at a house off South Wayne [Street], in the colored section near the creek," said Ellis. "We drove out there and found two women had been shot. …And there stood Marion Stembridge and Sam Terry, and Terry had a gun in his hand." Terry, a son of a former Baldwin County sheriff, had once been the county coroner. But since then, he had worked for Marion Stembridge, mostly as muscle to help with loan collections. His brother, oddly enough, had been Sarah Stembridge's first husband.[16]

One of the women Stembridge and Terry stood over was dead, the other wounded.

What exactly had led to the shooting remained murky even after Stembridge's later trial, but what had led Stembridge to the house was, for him, business as usual. A few months earlier, Stembridge had loaned Richard Cooper $800 to buy a 1941 Chevrolet. Stembridge had tacked an additional $227 onto the loan, ostensibly to insure the car. Cooper's mother, Emma Johnekin, and his brother cosigned the note. Cooper was to pay Stembridge $70 per month for 18 months; with the mother and brother obligated to pay an additional $15 monthly for reasons not clear. After a couple of months, Cooper's car was severely damaged in an accident and he approached Stembridge to have it repaired with the insurance. Stembridge, however, hadn't bothered to take out insurance. Cooper then stopped making payments, after which Stembridge repossessed the car and resold it. But Stembridge intended to continue collecting payments on the original loan. That day he had driven out to confront Cooper, taking along Terry.

Cooper wasn't home, so Stembridge confronted his mother. As was later claimed in court, he threatened Emma Johnekin with seizure of her furniture and other property if the payments weren't continued. In the ensuing argument, Stembridge pulled a gun and opened fire, hitting Johnekin four times and her sister once; the sister survived. At the approach of Ellis, Stembridge handed the gun to Terry. "I asked Terry later why he had taken it," said Ellis. "He said, 'With Marion, what would you have done?'"[17]

Stembridge claimed Terry had shot the women purely in self-defense, but Ellis's investigation gave the state solicitor, Shep Baldwin, reason to think otherwise. Both Stembridge and Terry were indicted for murder. That brought Stembridge and Ellis head-to-head for a second time.

"When I walked in his office that day he just looked at me," said Ellis. "He had crazy eyes that could stare right through you, but I could always stare him down. ... I told him, 'Mr. Stembridge, I've got a warrant for your arrest'. He said, 'Can I see the warrant?' and when I showed it he pulled a gun out of his desk."

Ellis leaped for Stembridge, wrestled the gun away, then handcuffed him and took him to jail. "He was raising hell the whole time," Ellis said, "saying how his rights were being violated. ... Shep Baldwin later told me the biggest mistake I ever made was not killin' him right then and there when he pulled the gun."

Stembridge was released on bond. For his part, Ellis kept a weather eye out for him. "I knew he hated my guts," Ellis said. "Crazy as he was, from then on he always beared watchin'."[18]

Marion Stembridge went to trial in July 1949, with Shep Baldwin prosecuting and Judge George Carpenter presiding. Marion Ennis defended Stembridge, having been persuaded to take the case by Roger Stembridge, whose wife was Ennis's cousin. Ennis, forty-two at the time, was one of the most prominent attorneys and civic leaders in Milledgeville. Besides being a star in the courtroom, he was a former and future state legislator, considered a worthy successor to Milledgeville's renowned state legislator Culver Kidd, and was even spoken of as a potential governor. Though the brothers were still not even speaking, Roger Stembridge had gotten his brother the best defender available.

Likely, though, no lawyer would have been good enough to get Stembridge off. The evidence against him was damning, and the best Ennis and his co-counsels – Jimmy Watts and Frank Evans – could do was concede to a charge of voluntary manslaughter. Stembridge was convicted and sentenced to from one to three years in prison. He appealed immediately, but dropped Ennis as his attorney. The appeals would drag on for three years and their finale would add yet another odd chapter to Stembridge's story. Sam Terry disappeared before the court date and was never tried.[19]

Out on bond awaiting his appeal, Stembridge abandoned his wife after a bare two years of marriage. The abandonment was nearly complete. As Sarah Stembridge later charged in her divorce filing, Stembridge continued to pay part of the utilities on the house they had shared, but she was forced to take a series of jobs – at the state hospital and, later, teaching in nearby towns – just to survive. Stembridge moved into the top floor of the Baldwin Hotel, and slowly more facets of his eccentricity seeped out into the community. He had a dozen locks and bolts put on the door of his room and would not allow the maids to clean the room unless he was there. He kept a large refrigerator in the room, padlocked. Rumors spread, likely originating from the maids, that he had put sheets of glass on the floor to guard against someone trying to electrocute him, and that he had put thin sheets of lead between the mattresses of his bed because he feared someone would try to kill him with X-rays. Other of his oddities were better founded than the local rumor mills. Robert Green, Stembridge's sometime attorney, also then lived at the Baldwin Hotel, which his older brother J.C. owned and managed. Green attested to one of Stembridge's minor oddities. "Newspapers were five cents apiece down at the front desk, but Marion wanted his to be in his letterbox," said Green. "If it wasn't, he would go up to his room and send down for one, always giving the bellhop 25 cents for it. ... Marion always wanted things his way."[20]

The next round of trouble for Stembridge was a lawsuit that also stemmed from his banking. The owner of the local brickyard sent one of his workers to attorney Eva Sloan with the request that she look into the man's case. Sloan worked with Marion Ennis and had for some time, first as his secretary and then, after passing the bar, his associate. The brickyard worker had borrowed $50 from Stembridge and after making payments for some time, had stopped. Stembridge had sued in small claims court to have the man's wages garnished. The man had never been served with court papers but Stembridge insisted on going ahead with the garnishment. Sloan discovered the man had already to that point paid $550 on the $50 loan. She countersued on the man's behalf and won; Stembridge was ordered to pay back the full $500 plus court costs. It was another blow to Stembridge's dubious banking business.

To Stembridge, losing the case was more than enough reason to hate both attorneys. Marion Ennis had now, by association, earned his second black mark in Stembridge's eyes, the first earned because Stembridge held Ennis in good part responsible for his manslaughter conviction.

Sloan had earned her first. Ironically, the first time the lives of Sloan and Stembridge had crossed, she had found him not altogether unpleasant. In the late 1930s and early 1940s, Sloan and her family had lived with Stembridge, renting one floor of his house while he lived on the other. He had kept very much to himself but he had seemed to like Sloan's three children, and liked to play with a pet dove they had found injured and nursed back to health. But by taking Stembridge to court – and winning – Sloan had clearly marked herself as his enemy.[21]

In July 1952, the U.S. Supreme Court rejected Stembridge's last appeal, and what followed baffled Milledgevillians, and frightened some. On September 6, Stembridge traveled with two lawyers – Victor

Davidson of Irwinton and George Jackson of Gray – to Wrightsville, in Johnson County, where at high noon he presented Sheriff Dewey Hall with papers assigning him to serve his sentence at that county's work camp.

Under ordinary circumstances, Stembridge should have been assigned to the state penitentiary, but Sheriff Hall found that the Georgia Department of Corrections had indeed sent Stembridge's paperwork to Johnson County. Immediately after Stembridge surrendered to Hall, Stembridge's lawyers filed a request with Johnson County Superior Court Judge Roy Rowland that Stembridge be released on grounds of habeas corpus, charging the testimony that convicted him was perjured.

The judge set the hearing for 2:00 p.m. and the five men – Stembridge, his lawyers, the sheriff, and the judge – went to lunch, together. At 2:00 p.m., Judge Rowland granted the motion for habeas corpus. Marion Stembridge was a free man.

After Stembridge's death, the circumstances of his release provoked an inconclusive investigation by the state bar association and various committees of the legislature, which pronounced the release as "unheard of before in Georgia." To some Milledgevillians, the release seemed to indicate the awesome degree to which Stembridge could use his wealth to buy influence at high levels. "I don't think they ever figured out how he did it," said Eugene Ellis. Stembridge seemed a man who could get away with anything. Or thought he could.[22]

### Wind Up To The End And The Final Act

That arrogance was the mainspring of his next round of troubles. By late 1952, his various dealings had attracted the attention of the Internal Revenue Service. IRS investigators determined that Stembridge had not filed tax returns some years and when he had filed, had evidently substantially underreported his income. In late December, IRS agents Julian Odum and Yancey Edwards approached Stembridge in his store and informed him he would be charged with tax evasion. According to testimony at his later trial, he offered the agents $10,000 to make his problems disappear. They told him they would consider it and come back later.

On January 6, 1953, they returned and told him they had mulled it over and would cover up his evasion for $10,000 each. Stembridge claimed he didn't have that kind of money, but when the men appeared to hem and haw, he went into the back of the store and came out with $20,000 in two stacks. The agents were wearing microphones, however, and Stembridge had charged headlong into their sting. He was arrested for tax evasion and attempted bribery. His trial was set for the April term of federal court in Macon.[23]

According to Eva Sloan's later account, Stembridge believed that she and Marion Ennis had set the IRS on him. They hadn't, but Stembridge's hatred for them was stoked just the same.

In March, Sarah Stembridge added to Marion's mounting troubles by deciding to make her break from him permanent. She filed for divorce, alleging as her main reasons Marion's "willful and continued desertion, his conviction for "a crime of moral turpitude" (his 1949 manslaughter conviction), and "cruel treatment." In expanding on the last, she alleged, among others, that he had kept her as a "virtual slave" working at his business and in their home; that he forbade her to visit friends and relatives; that he continually heaped profane and vile abuse upon her; and that he was prone to "fits of temper and rages of anger" during which he would shove, kick, and slap her. She lived, she said, in constant fear of him.

She further added to the townspeople's catalogue of Stembridge's oddities when she claimed he slept with a gun under his pillow, and that during the time they actually had lived together, whenever she served their meals he would switch their plates out of fear she would poison him. In his answer, Stembridge denied her allegations of abuse and made similar claims of abuse against her, with many references to "nagging and fussing."

To locals, it seemed the final wrapping had been torn from the strange life of the man who was becoming Milledgeville's most notorious citizen. For their part, they were actually inclined to believe the claims of both Stembridges.[24]

Sarah Stembridge engaged a law firm in a neighboring town to handle her divorce, but the firm hired Milledgeville attorney Stephen "Pete" Bivens to shepherd the case. Bivens, twenty-seven, was a star graduate of Milledgeville's Georgia Military College and of Cornell University. He was widely regarded as one of the city's rising leaders.

Bivens had already courted Stembridge's hatred by taking a case for a client contesting a mortgage foreclosure. Stembridge had evidently sworn a false oath in the course of filing the foreclosure and Bivens pressed for an indictment for perjury. Now Stembridge had another reason to hate him. According to Robert Green, at least four attorneys in Milledgeville warned Bivens to "go easy on Stem" because he was unstable. Bivens's answer to each warning was that he carried a Colt .45 in his pocket and wasn't worried about Stembridge.[25]

In April, Marion Stembridge went to trial in Macon's federal court. During the trial Stembridge loudly denounced the "courthouse crowd" in Milledgeville that he claimed was "all against him" and responsible for his troubles.

But on Monday, April 27, a jury deliberated for only fifty minutes before convicting him of tax evasion and the two counts of attempted bribery of federal agents. Judge A.B. Conger gave him one week to get his affairs in order and ordered him to report the next Monday, May 4, for sentencing.

Stembridge filed his own appeal for the convictions, and then, according to Robert Green, "holed up in his room for three days."

On Friday, May 1, he mailed two large bound and locked suitcases to a sister in Washington, D.C. He also visited Marion Ennis's office several times, but Ennis was away on a trip to Macon to promote Milledgeville's sesquicentennial celebration, set to begin the next day.[26]

What Stembridge did on that last morning before he went up to Marion Ennis's office was pieced together afterward. He borrowed the car of a woman who sometimes worked as his secretary, a woman about whom Milledgevillians later could recall little except that she had only one leg. He drove first out of Milledgeville to the home of Shep Baldwin, who had prosecuted him in 1949. Baldwin was in his home that morning watching television and saw Stembridge drive into his yard. Stembridge paused but never got out of the car; he then drove on. Baldwin's wife had driven his car into town that morning, and Baldwin later opined that Stembridge, not seeing the car, had assumed he wasn't home.

Stembridge arrived back in town and parked in the lot of the Piggly Wiggly grocery store, across from the courthouse and behind the Sanford Building. He left the car's door open and the engine running, maybe in readiness for a getaway, maybe just a preoccupied oversight.

He walked to the courthouse, where some later recalled he looked at the closed windows of the office of Judge George Carpenter, probably assuming the closed windows on the warm morning meant the judge wasn't in. (He wasn't.) On several occasions before that morning, the judge had called Eugene Ellis about anonymous telephoned death threats that he suspected came from Marion Stembridge.[27]

Stembridge went to the office of J.C. Cooper, clerk of the superior court, who had handled all the paperwork for the many legal proceedings against him. Cooper was in. When Stembridge entered, Cooper looked up from his desk and said, "Hello, Mr. Stembridge." Stembridge stared but said nothing. He just propped open the office door and left. Cooper later opined, probably rightly, that Stembridge had marked him for death as well, but evidently considered him a low priority.[28]

Marion Ennis and Eva Sloan were in their offices located above the Campus Theater movie emporium that morning, too. Usually they would not have been, but Ennis was also the county attorney and he and Sloan were preparing checks for county employees before a county commission meeting set for later that morning. Ordinarily, the commission would have met the following Tuesday, but with the sesquicentennial festivities planned for the full week, the meeting had been moved to Saturday.

At a little after 10 a.m., Ennis and Sloan were already late for the meeting, but nearly finished.

Campus Theater as in current days. The law offices of Stembridge's victims were above.(author photo)

While Ennis took a telephone call, Sloan stepped up the hall to the office of attorney Lee Parttiss, where conversation quickly turned to Marion Stembridge's conviction five days before. Sloan's back was to the door. Suddenly, Parttiss put his finger to his lips, signaling her to be quiet. He had just seen Stembridge walk down the hall toward Ennis's office.

Both then heard loud pops, but, curiously, were neither alarmed nor surprised, since both thought it was simply the firecrackers some were setting off in the toy muskets down on the street. Evidently, the single-minded Stembridge never noticed Sloan in Parttiss's office. Only that oversight kept her alive.

When she walked back down to the office, Sloan no way expected what she found. Ennis was lying on his stomach, bleeding. He had been shot three times. As the coroner's inquest would later show, Stembridge's first bullet had hit Ennis in his shoulder, the second in his stomach. A probably lethal wound, but not enough for Stembridge. With Ennis collapsed on the floor, Stembridge had then stood over him and fired another .45 caliber slug into his back. The panicked Sloan knelt over Ennis. He raised his head and tried to speak, but blood gushed from his mouth. He died grasping Sloan's arm; she had to pry his hand loose to rise. Everyone in the office suites was alerted now. A woman yelled to the street below that Ennis was shot. A chiropractor told that he had seen Stembridge run by his office, toward the stairs.[29]

Robert Green saw Stembridge soon after his sometime client entered the Sanford Building. A woman had walked into Green's office looking for the chiropractor's office and Green was directing her to the offices above the Campus Theater when he saw Stembridge outside his door. Green thought that odd. Stembridge had never come to his office before, always sending the paperwork when he had work for him. But Stembridge walked on past without so much as a glance. Pete Bivens's office was down the hall.[30]

When Stembridge entered that office, Bivens was dictating a letter to his secretary, Jean Stockum. According to Stockum's later testimony to the coroner's jury, when Bivens saw him, he said, "Good morning, Mr. Stembridge, what can I do for you?" Without a word, Stembridge opened fire. He emptied his Colt 1911 .45 cal. semi-automatic, all four remaining shots hitting Bivens in the chest. Between the first and last shots, Bivens rose and started for Stembridge. When Bivens reached him, Stembridge was frantically trying to slam another magazine into his gun. Bivens managed to wrest the gun and ammunition from him, but slumped to the floor after reaching the hall, the gun pinned under him. Stembridge hurried toward the stairs leading down to the back door.[31]

Green and his accidental visitor heard the shots and Stockum's screams. Green's visitor became hysterical and Green shoved her under his desk and began telephoning the police and for an ambulance. In an instant he formed a good idea what had just happened. Then Green heard another shot.

When it seemed the shooting was over, Green entered the hall. He saw Bivens lying face down with a local doctor kneeling over him. Green was met by Deputy Sheriff Buford Lingo, who told him what had happened and that he should take the woman to safety.[32]

From the time Stembridge walked up the stairs of the Campus Theater, it had all played out in less than twenty minutes.

For Ellis, the end of all the shooting was only a beginning. He had to try to make sense of it all. One place to try was Stembridge's room in the Baldwin Hotel. After getting through all the locks, Ellis found the room as rumor had described it, and more. In each corner of the room were loaded guns and ammunition. On the nightstand beside Stembridge's bed was a Bible and – something that gives Ellis an ironic chuckle to this day – a copy of the book *How to Win Friends and Influence People*.

Only when Ellis went to Stembridge's office did it all start to make sense. On Stembridge's desk he found a handwritten suicide note:

*May 1, 1953*

*To whom it may concern:*

*I just do not care to be sentenced for another crime I did not commit. In this connection, I will not be able to do my full duty. I can only do the best that I can.*

*Marion W. Stembridge*

*I was convicted by tampering with the jury.*

What Stembridge evidently saw as his "duty" was to kill as many of his perceived tormentors as he could before ending his own life. Certainly he wanted Ennis and Bivens dead, and Eva Sloan lived only because she had stepped down the hall moments before Stembridge entered the Campus Theater building. But exactly how many others he hoped to kill is uncertain. Shep Baldwin and Judge Carpenter, almost certainly; Cooper, probably; perhaps Sarah Stembridge; and maybe even Eugene Ellis. "He would've killed me if he could," said Ellis. "He hated me enough."

One clue to Stembridge's full plans may be that he was carrying eight spare magazines for his Colt .45 semi-automatic, plus the .38 cal. revolver. Over the weeks afterward, rumors circulated around Milledgeville that Stembridge had a "death list" in his pocket naming those he planned to kill, but according to Ellis no list was ever found. And despite his leaving his car running, clearly Stembridge never thought he could run very far or for very long. Coupled with his previous visits to Ennis's office, the Friday date on the suicide note indicates he likely had intended to carry out the murders the day before.[33]

The parade scheduled for that Saturday afternoon was canceled, but the grand ball went on as planned. Both Ennis and Bivens had been on the sesquicentennial planning committee and their families agreed both men would have wanted the town's anticipated revelries to go on.

The full week of events went on, interrupted only by the three funerals. The service for Stembridge was sparsely attended. According to Eva Sloan, the murders were little discussed during the sesquicentennial because "everyone was trying hard to make the celebration perfect." Dealing with the tragedy could come afterward.[34]

Part of dealing with it all was cleaning up the details, which included pulling the final wrappings off Marion Stembridge's life. There would be, in the final accounting, almost as many more questions as answers about what had happened – and why. There were no ready answers to be found.

Over half a century later, most of these questions still linger.

In Stembridge's store, Ellis and others found five locked safes. Locksmiths were called in the crack the safes. Fearing the safes were boobytrapped, Ellis and Dennis Cox blocked off the downtown streets as a precaution. When the safes were opened, some contained jars and jugs of urine bearing Stembridge's name and dates, and instructions that if he should die the samples were to be tested for poisons. Rusty nails and parts of guns were found in some of the safes. Milledgeville jeweler John W. Grant opened one safe and found in it an M-1 carbine rifle.

What wasn't found was Marion Stembridge's much rumored money. Later, townspeople speculated that what cash Stembridge had on hand he had mailed to his sister in the two suitcases. This speculation was never confirmed, however.[35]

A few days after the killings, J.C. Green, owner of the Baldwin Hotel, delivered to his brother Robert a letter posted from Stembridge. According to Robert Green, J.C. Green was one of the few people Marion Stembridge had ever seemed to trust and the letter contained another sealed letter that Stembridge instructed be delivered to his relatives. Robert Green arranged the delivery, but said the Stembridge family never revealed what the sealed letter contained.[36]

When Stembridge's will was probated, his wife was left one dollar, the absolute minimum under Georgia law, though later in court she was awarded the house she had shared with Marion. She remained in Milledgeville for a short time before moving away.

The rest of his estate Stembridge left to his sisters, who sold off most of his property. When the goods of the store were auctioned, Eugene Ellis bought Stembridge's desk, the same that Stembridge had been sitting behind the day Ellis had arrested him. "For some reason I just wanted that desk," said Ellis. He used it in his own office for years.[37]

When the final details were wrapped up, Milledgevillians got on with trying to both deal with their loss and put the whole matter behind them. Maybe the best expression of the town's sentiments were in the epitaph Milledgeville *Union-Recorder* editor Jere Moore wrote for Marion Ennis. After outlining Ennis's virtues and record of community service, Moore wrote, "Marion Stembridge leaves no act to be remembered by except the crime he so cunningly committed after premeditated planning in detail." To many Milledgevillians, Marion Ennis and Pete Bivens had represented the best of the town, Marion Stembridge the worst. Perhaps the unspoken consensus in the years afterward to say little about the incident was just an attempt to forget the worst.[38]

There is a hero in the story of Marion Stembridge, however, and it is a quiet, unassuming one named Eugene Ellis. He was never reluctant to talk about Stembridge and is just as willing today. He tells the story with little emotion, in his acquired middle Georgia accent with rolling "r"s that betray his New England upbringing. It was just another case to him, he says, and he means it. He had a thoroughly honorable career by any standard, but considers it as his just having done his job. He was police chief of Milledgeville until 1974 and never had an unsolved murder case. Among others, he captured multi-state serial killer John Paul Knowles in 1974, a case he worked with his then-investigator James Jossey.

One exploit Ellis is reluctant to speak of in detail, though, is when he was, in effect, deputized by the CIA to keep an eye on the wife of Francis Gary Powers and her mother. The famous U-2 pilot's wife lived in Milledgeville during the time Powers was a prisoner in the Soviet Union.

After retiring from the police department, Ellis served for nine years as chief deputy of the Baldwin County Sheriff's Department. To him it was all just doing a job he loved.

His greatest pride seems to come from his sons following in his footsteps. His son Randy is a career veteran of the county sheriff's department. His son George began his own career as a dispatcher for police department, and later joined the highway patrol. In 2000, George Ellis was named the Georgia State Patrol's commander, carrier of Badge No. 1.

His badge now long laid aside, Eugene Ellis fills his time with his trains. At sixteen, his first job was as a railroad telegrapher and he never lost his love of the rails. He gives one room of his house over to an intricate electric train layout running through a finely detailed and panoramic landscape in miniature of Milledgeville as it has appeared over the years. Each detailed building is the product of hours of craftsmanship. He doesn't dwell on his old cases, he says, but he does keep one souvenir of that awful day in May 1953. Marion Stembridge's handwritten suicide note. Which he takes out to look at from time to time.

Eugene Ellis, with one memento of the Stembridge case that he has kept over the years, Stembridge's suicide note. A second artifact was Stembridge's desk, which Ellis used during his later years as Milledgeville's police chief.

# 7

# From A Georgia Chain Gang To The Great Escape

George Harsh didn't like his new job. He didn't like anything about it or want anything to do with it.

Leaders of the escape committee of Stalag Luft III planned a tunneling breakout of over two hundred prisoners and they told Harsh he was in charge of the operation's security. It was crackpot scheme, he told them, sure to get them all killed. But he was an officer in the Canadian Royal Air Force, and orders were orders.

"But why me?" Harsh later asked his friend Canadian flier Wally Floody, a member of the escape planning organization. Surely among the hundreds of prisoners languishing in these barbwired barrens hacked out of the woodlands outside Sagan, in the German province of Silesia, there were other candidates for the job of keeping tabs on the movements and snooping of their German guards.

"Oh yeah," said Floody, smiling. "And how many of them have spent twelve years in prison? We need a man on this job with some experience.

"You know something," Floody said, chuckling. "You're probably the only man in the world ever to get a job because he's an ex-convict."[1]

In a life with more lows that highs to that point, Harsh would eventually take both his predicament as a prisoner and the task he had been volunteered for – ordered to do – all in stride. As in so many other instances since he had been twenty-one years old, there wasn't much choice left to him. After all, through his eyes he had had few real choices since his decisions that had landed him first a death sentence and then life on a Georgia chain gang without chance of parole.

George Rutherford Harsh, Jr. was only thirty-four years old in early 1943 when he was dragooned into running the complex security operation for the breakout from Stalag Luft III that books and films have immortalized as "The Great Escape." But he was grayheaded and had an air of worldliness and hard living that gave most the impression he was older. That was a deep-dyeing of his criminal and prison youth, with all the experiences of that seamy side of the world. And he had lived hard. Originally, he'd been sentenced at age eighteen to death in the electric chair for two "thrill kills," as the press of 1928-29 dubbed them, murders during a crime spree with a cohort of drinking buddies while a student at Oglethorpe University in Atlanta. His sentence was commuted to life in prison, through the influence of money he later wrote, though publicly it came as part of a deal for his partner-in-crime's confession. It was a salvation he sometimes regretted during his first years that were spent in a brutal chain gang camp. The experience steeled him, though, he later realized, for everything that happened to him after he ultimately won his freedom. And that included his time behind German barbed wire as a key member of the camp's escape apparatus, codenamed by the prisoners the "X Organization."

### Silver Spoon Childhood, Troubled Youth

George Rutherford Harsh was born in Milwaukee, Wisconsin in 1909, the son of a wealthy shoe manufacturer. At his father's death in 1921, the then twelve-year-old George Jr., called "Junie" by his family was endowed with a trust fund of $500,000. When both prosecutors and his defense attorneys assembled profiles of Harsh years later – the defense attorneys trying to make a case for diminished capacity or insanity – what they found was a portrait of a boy intellectually gifted in some ways, a lover of poetry recitals in fact, with a fine pedigree and the social varnish to set it off, but whose character owed a great deal, perhaps, to too much money and too little affection.

Or perhaps a skewed kind of affection, that of his mother coming with a probably unhealthy dose of overindulgence and none coming from a father figure. Certainly since the death his father was he was remembered by the principal and teachers of his preparatory school as moody, and with a quick and violent temper when challenged.[2]

In 1923, Harsh's mother withdrew him from school and the two traveled around the world, both just for the sake of doing it and for the tall and thin George's health, which his mother believed delicate. As his later profile showed, it was during this trip that the fourteen-year-old George developed his taste for liquor. Harsh, one of the doctors who examined him before his trial testified, "discovered that alcohol makes the world look rosy. ... It helped him forget a chronic disposition to feel inferior." The statement given by one Harsh's chums of the time is more pointed: Junie Harsh , "was the type of boy who, when drunk, was mean and nasty instead of foolish or high-spirited." At the same time, however, he was passionately devoted to his mother, always wanting to appear in his best light in her eyes. He would drink, one friend recalled for investigators, but he would drive around until he sobered up because, he told the friend, "I'll make mother feel badly if she sees me this way."[3]

Harsh attended another preparatory school in Asheville, North Carolina, for a short time before enrolling in Oglethorpe University in Atlanta. He was suspected at first of plagiarizing his entering essay, until he demonstrated to the faculty the almost phenomenal writing ability and style that he was to demonstrate years later in his memoirs. And this, together with a great deal of worldly knowledge gleaned from his travels. But the portrait of him at this time is also, on top of his other sometimes moody, sometimes tumultuous tendencies, shows him acquiring a certain worldly cynicism and stoicism that could make him appear cold, completely devoid of any emotion at times when others might break down. Reporters who interviewed him after his arrest described him as polite and affable, greeting them with "Good to see you," and willing to talk about his crimes, expressing deep remorse. But he showed no emotion at his trial, and when hearing his death sentence, the *Atlanta Journal* reported, "There was not a tremor to indicate stress, nor the slightest twitching of the hands, nor the heightening of color in his face."[4]

It had started as a lark, as Harsh later recounted in his memoir over forty years later. A foolishly dangerous prank and experiment that got out of hand. At Oglethorpe University he fell in with a steady group of four others much like himself, all from "well-to-do families and two of the families were 'families of position.'" Of course, one of those was his own Milwaukee family; the other was that of Richard Gray Gallogly, from a family near the very top of Atlanta society. Gallogly's grandfather was James R. Gray, owner of the *Atlanta Journal*, one of the most influential newspapers in the South, with Atlanta's WSB radio also part of the family holdings. It was a family, however, of which Richard Gallogly, dubbed "Dapper Dick" in the press after his arrest, was clearly the family wastrel, well-dressed, well-mannered and a bitter disappointment. Perhaps even a psychopath. He, Harsh and the others, including Harsh's roommate and fellow Kappa Alpha pledge at Oglethorpe, Jack Mahoney, pursued bootleg liquor in Prohibition-era Atlanta's roadhouses more diligently than they pursued studies.

### Pursuing The Perfect Crime

One night in the fall of 1928, the five sat around a table in a roadhouse, a gallon of corn liquor in the center of the table fueling their "bull session," as Harsh later described it, and their thoughts turned to crime.

In his memoir Harsh never named Gallogly as the instigator of their crime spree, just as he refused to testify against Gallogly at Gallogly's own trial, even after implicating Gallogly in his own confession. But other accounts do indeed lay the hatching of the fateful idea squarely at the feet of the Atlanta dandy.

It is difficult to be certain, though, how truthful Harsh is about this in his memoirs, and whether his obviously deliberate use of the third person is intended to further equivocate on Gallogly's behalf or his own. In any case, the talk of that night would change their lives forever and for the worse.[5]

"...One boy advanced the idea that it was possible to commit the perfect crime, that all that was needed was careful planning, organization and intelligence," Harsh recounted. "He maintained that five people of some education, by pooling their brains and carefully plotting and making provisions for every contingency, could outwit the police, whom he contended had their hands full anyway. He actually made his arguments sound plausible. Prior to that night I am certain the idea of deliberately setting out to commit a crime just to prove that it could be done was one of the farthest things from my mind," Harsh wrote. "This held true for all the others around that table — except one."

"One of the boys," in Harsh's telling, went to his car and returned with a Colt .45 cal. semi-automatic pistol and laid it in the center of the table. It was one of the ugliest weapons ever devised, the young man said, but also one of the most efficient. It was his contention, he added, that with such a weapon "a determined man can be the master of any situation. ..." "He talked well, this young man, he talked convincingly and he hammered home his points," Harsh recalled. "And he had the mysterious quality called leadership."[6]

Over the next few weeks the area around Atlanta became the playground of the five "Polite Bandits," as the sensational press wasn't long in dubbing them. The string of armed robberies, seven in all, as Harsh later wrote, 'left the police running in circles" and the newspapers screaming for blood.

As Harsh later described their method, the five would draw straws before each robbery, with the short straw and his chosen confederate traveling in one car to the scene of the coming robbery that the five had previously scouted. The other three would travel along in another car, ready to run interference on any pursuers during the getaway. The gang's takes varied from a few dollars to several hundred, but the amount of the loot mattered far less than the act of robbing itself. Newspaper accounts quoted witnesses as remarking how cool and confident, and how well-dressed and, yes, polite the young robbers were. The moniker "Polite Bandits" followed quickly and naturally.

Through it all, too, they remained focused on the end result. "We're learning our trade," Harsh quotes the "leader" (again, certainly Gallogly) as saying at some point. "And we're proving our point. Very soon we'll wind this thing up by knocking over a bank I've been casing for some time. It'll be easy ... and then we can quit. And we can live out the rest of our lives knowing that the perfect crime has been committed."[7]

But things actually had started to go wrong for the boys as early as their second venture. That robbery was on the night of October 6, a cold, rainy night with the wind gusting, blowing the rain in sheets, Harsh later recalled, with few people on the streets and those few interested only in getting home. "It was," Harsh wrote of it, "an ideal night for petty hold up men, muggers and punks generally." Their target was an A&P grocery at 1004 Hemphill Avenue.

"I had drawn the short straw," Harsh recounted, "and twice we drove past the cased target for this foray." Only two clerks could be seen, in Harsh's account. Other accounts have up to ten customers in the store. In any case, when the two cars of the gang stopped around the corner, Harsh alighted and entered, announcing loudly that it was a hold up, "barked in as steady a voice as I could manage."

One clerk, actually the store manager, I.V. Ellis, was at the bend of the U-shaped counters tallying the days' receipts, while the other clerk, to Harsh's left, was restocking shelves.

That clerk, S.H. Meeks by name, "slowly raised his hands, an open-mouthed look of terror on his face," but then Ellis snatched a .38 caliber revolver from under the counter and began firing – "…deciding to be a hero for someone else's money," as Harsh put it.

Harsh began firing, purely on reflex, he later said, firing three shots, all of which hit Ellis, wounding him in the left arm and the right leg. Some versions of the story circulated later have Harsh entering with his gun blazing, but that would have been counter to the usual practice of the "Polite Bandits." It is, though, perhaps an indicator of how the boys' crime wave gripped the city at the time. But in whatever version, the air still ended up full of high-caliber lead. Ellis's last spasmodic shot sent a .38 slug to wing Harsh in a hip. One of his shots intended for Harsh hit Meeks. Ellis would survive, but Meeks would die the next day. In his memoirs, Harsh would inaccurately recall that both died.

Curiously, he would also relate the story as the gang's last robbery. His wound, in any case, was minor, and didn't deter him from further adventures.[8]

The gang's last raid, on October 16, was on Smith's Drug Store, at the corner of 10th Street and what is now Monroe Drive in Atlanta. When the holdup was announced, twenty-four year-old pharmacist Willard Smith pulled a pistol and began firing. The story of the A&P holdup had rippled through the Atlanta merchant community and Smith is reported to have declared to friends that if his pharmacy were targeted he intended to fight.

Again the drawer of the short straw, Harsh returned Smith's fire and Smith took a .45 cal. slug through a lung. He would die five days later. One of Smith's bullets had also found its target, however, ripping through the fleshy part of Harsh's groin.[9]

"As I limped out to the waiting cars, I could feel the warm blood running down my leg and squishing in my shoe," Harsh recalled. "Right at that moment in my life I was a terrified young punk with a hole in my groin out of which my blood was pouring. If I didn't die from that wound, I knew a hangman's noose was waiting for me … or worse yet, a prison cell for the rest of my life." But he also recalled at that moment feeling anger that the pharmacist had fought back.[10]

What happened next Harsh glossed over his in memoir, perhaps even over forty years after the fact intentionally hazing the account to avoid implicating any of the rest of the gang.

His compatriots drove him to an apartment on 16th Street. Here again, accounts vary. Harsh identifies it as Gallogly's apartment. Other versions identify it as that of a friend of Harsh's, Jack Wright. Whichever is true, there they called another friend of Harsh's, Dr. Julian Riley, to whom they explained the wound as resulting from some playful scuffling over a gun. Riley carried Harsh to St. Joseph's hospital.

Harsh stayed overnight in the hospital before going to Gallogly's family home for a few days of recovery before returning to his dormitory at the university. He explained his limp as resulting from his breaking a liquor bottle while it was in his pocket.

Given Harsh's reputation on campus, it was a canny and plausible story. Harsh found, however, that in his own thoughts he couldn't lie away the truth.[11]

## Caught

"The ghastly reality and the tragic consequences of what we were doing crashed into the awareness of us all," Harsh remembered. The gun was hidden and the crime wave halted "and five young men began to realize that what they had done in their youth would follow them for the rest of their lives." As it turned out, the consequences weren't far behind, after an unlucky break.

Gallogly and Jack Mahoney had disposed of Harsh's bloody shirt and underclothes in Peachtree Creek, but they had missed his pants. These were left rolled up on the floor of a closet, where they were found by Gallogly's maid. She sent them out to Gallogly's dry cleaner. The dry cleaner, spotting the hole in the bloody pants, called the police. Detective John W. Lowe, who had been assigned the A&P robbery case, traced another cleaner's laundry mark on the pants back to Harsh's own cleaner. Lowe obtained warrants for both Harsh and Gallogly. On October 27, a chilly Saturday, Harsh was walking at the corner of Peachtree Street and North Avenue, heading for that day's football game between Georgia Tech and North Carolina, when Lowe and another officer, who reportedly knew Harsh by sight, arrested him.

In his memoirs, Harsh recounted that his confession was beaten out of him over about an hour by Atlanta Police detective chief Lamar Poole, wielding a rubber hose. "...After I had picked myself up off the floor for the fourth time, it seemed pointless to keep repeating like a parrot, 'I have nothing to say.' After all, the holes in the suit matched the holes in me ... and there was that rubber hose."

Police accounts are, naturally, quite different. "We had not been together five minutes before Harsh started to confess," John Lowe told a reporter a few days after the arrest. "We got from him every criminal move he has made since the first of this month, when he started his life of lawlessness." The investigators claimed that Harsh, confronted with the bloody pants, readily admitted the seven robberies and two killings, and that he also readily implicated Gallogly.

That worthy was picked up later that same day in Athens, where he had attended the University of Georgia's homecoming football game. In his car, police found the Colt .45 cal. semi-automatic. Unlike

Harsh, however, Gallogly admitted nothing, and through his family called in a battery of attorneys, with his principal attorney Reuben Arnold.[12]

The sensationalist media wasn't long in dubbing them "thrill killers" and comparing them to Nathan Leopold and Richard Loeb, two Chicago youth of wealthy families who had killed a young boy in 1924 simply for the experience and to see if they could get away with it. Legendary attorney Clarence Darrow had managed to spare Leopold and Loeb the death penalty, getting them life sentences, but Darrow had had one advantage: neither of his clients had ever confessed.

Harsh's attorney, former Georgia congressman William Schley Howard, who with Reuben Arnold had been defense counsel to accused murderer Leo Frank in an infamously sensational 1913 case, had a client who had admitted his crimes.

Howard had one long chance to play, and that was to seek a verdict of not guilty by reason of insanity.

When Howard hired six practitioners of the then fairly young science of psychiatry to examine Harsh, the state prosecutor, John Boykin, engaged another six. For three weeks, as Harsh later recalled, "these twelve psychiatrists picked, probed, tested and analyzed me." The examination included extensive X-rays of his head, looking for evidence of any kind of injury that could have damaged his brain. In the end, Harsh recounted, the two separate reports by the two separate teams of doctors concluded exactly the same thing: "I was as sane as they were."[13]

He was also talkative, feeling he had nothing more at that point to hide, readily granting interviews to newspaper reporters visiting him in the Fulton County jail, but expressing remorse. "We were just out drinking, stewed to the gills and looking for fun," he told one reporter. "I am deeply sorry ...I have brought upon myself great calamity, but I have no one to blame but myself. I know that a confession will not do any good to those whose lives have been darkened by the acts of me and my partner. But I have made a complete confession, and I will stand by it for better or worse."

On another occasion he explained his confession by saying, "Everything that I can undo I am trying to undo. I only wish I could undo the rest." Gallogly, for his part, kept his mouth shut, refusing to discuss any aspect of the charges against him.

Harsh's trial began on January 15, 1929 and lasted four days.

William Howard used everything in his arsenal. A total of ten medical experts for both the state and the defense testified on various aspects of the tests that had been done on Harsh.

State prosecutor Boykin tried to show that Harsh and Gallogly had robbed and killed for both the thrill and for money, needed by the spendthrifts who had a habit of quickly burning through their allowances.

A defense co-counsel even tried to blame a portion of Harsh's supposed mental turbulences on the local moonshine he had drunk, which the attorney claimed was full of potash.

Observers noted that Harsh sat through it all with his air of apparent indifference, showing no emotion. To a few, this seemed evidence that Harsh lacked normal human impulses such as empathy and compassion, the lack of these considered a sign of mental illness.

Howard sought to turn Harsh's evident attitude to advantage in his remarks to the jury. "We went to that jail and talked with this boy," Howard said. "We asked him why he did it, and he said he didn't know. He showed absolutely no emotional reactions, and we came away convinced that the crime he committed was not that of a sane man."

Howard was among the most skilled defense attorneys in the state, and he had won many cases and would win many more, but on this occasion his oratory and legal legerdemain couldn't sell George Harsh in any state of mind as an innocent man. The jury was out fifteen minutes before returning its verdict: guilty as charged. Judge E.D. Thomas duly sentenced Harsh to death in the electric chair, with a tentative execution date of March 15. Howard immediately filed an appeal.[14]

**Spared The Chair**

Gallogly's trial began on January 29. Harsh refused to testify. Neither of the two ever implicated any of their other gang members, even Jack Mahoney, who was arrested in the case but never charged. Gallogly readily admitted that the Colt .45 cal. semi-automatic used in the robberies and shootings was his, but he asserted that Harsh, who he described as often drunk, had been the instigator of the crimes and that he, Gallogly, had on occasions tried to stop him.

Witnesses from the robberies placed Gallogly at the scenes but could not agree on what parts he had played. Nothing substantial could really shake his account that Harsh was the principal actor in their drama.

In explaining the eventual result of the trial some have also looked at the role Gallogly's family and its influence might have had. It's often pointed out in accounts of the trial, for example, that Hoke Smith, the one-time Secretary of the Interior under President Grover Cleveland, later Georgia's governor and U.S. senator, who had sold the *Atlanta Journal* to Gallogly's grandfather, sat with Gallogly's mother and appeared on close terms Gallogly himself, even sitting between them on occasion.

In any event, the jury deadlocked on Gallogly's guilt, six to six, and a mistrial was declared.

So, too, at the second trial.

On the eve of the third trial, Gallogly and his lawyers offered a deal. He would plead guilty in return for a mandatory life sentence instead of the death penalty, if Harsh could also be spared death by receiving the same sentence.

It was a curious offer to make, it would seem in the wrap up, and can only be explained as an act of loyalty to Harsh, a brand of loyalty that had so far in the case been most shown by Harsh. Still, "Dapper Dick" played more gallant than remorseful. He wasn't guilty of murder and didn't believe he would be convicted, Gallogly maintained in his statement, but his sole interest was to help Harsh, whom Gallogly claimed had acted "under the influence of liquor to the extent that he did not take my advice to stay out of the drugstore."[15]

Boykin agreed to the deal if Judge Thomas would agree to set aside his original sentence and accept Harsh's plea as well. Thomas did. In his memoirs, Harsh called it a practical decision on the judge's part, though lending it what was his customary cynical coloring. "There's an old saying in this country, 'you can't hang a million dollars';" he wrote. With the money that both his and Gallogly's family could call on, he said, one could "keep two cases in court until the defendants died of old age. Judge Thomas knew this."[16]

Harsh had no illusions that he wasn't, perhaps, escaping true justice, or as he later put it: "Had I received justice I would have been hanged as high as Haman, and with a length of rusty barbed wire." At the time, however, he played to his cohort's script, expressing his gratitude to Gallogly. "It was a most magnanimous act, after two mistrials, for him to come to my rescue this way," Harsh said from his jail cell. "Dick is not guilty of any murder. It is a great thing to have a friend who would do what he has done for me."[17]

Perhaps Harsh's hazing of the events of the time in his memoirs sprang from a genuine desire to forget the details. (It's unlikely that he actually did forget. His memoir of chockful of fine vivid details recounted decades after their appearance in Harsh's story.) Or perhaps in downplaying Gallogly's role he considered it payback on a debt. In any case, their stories split after their pleas, not to rejoin until January 1941, when both were pardoned by then Gov. E.D. Rivers.

(Harsh's pardon would be justified, as we will see, but it's difficult to pinpoint anything in Gallogly's history that earned him the same consideration.)

Gallogly did not adapt to prison as well as Harsh, by all accounts. His record includes at least one suicide attempt, in 1932, and hospitalization for a nervous breakdown in 1939. His transport from the hospital provided the avenue for his escape to Texas in the personal car of the Georgia state prison inspector, one of the more celebrated escapes in Georgia penal history, but he was recaptured in March 1940.

After his release, the once aspiring prince of crime lived a quiet life, except for a drunk driving conviction in 1943, and died in June 2002.

### Working on the chain gang

Harsh's home for much of the next seven years was one of the last of the "cage camp" chain gangs in southern Georgia. The name came from the thirty rusting iron cages on wheels drawn up into a rough circle, looking to Harsh "like the forlorn and abandoned remnants of a tawdry circus."

At one time, the cages had formed a moveable prison camp, hauling and quartering the chain gang wherever the state's work took them, but now the wagons, canvas-covered in winter, housed the prisoners year-round inside a roughly two-acre compound of "hard-packed Georgia red clay soil" enclosed by barbed wire. Two shacks, one a combination kitchen and mess hall and the other a latrine, completed the tableau, home for about 240 prisoners.

In the summers, in Harsh's recollection, red dust covered everything and gave it a hellish look. In the winters, the place swam in red mud.[18]

If Harsh fudged any of the details of his crimes in his memoirs, he was unsparing in his descriptions of life on the chain gang. One of the first things he had to do, very common to young prisoners, was fend off the advance of an older homosexual prisoner seeking to lay his claim on the new arrival. Most prisoners, he wrote, did not abandon their natural heterosexuality. It was considered an abandonment of hope of ever leading a normal life. But some prisoners did, about thirty to forty out of the 240 in Harsh's estimation. Many of the older of these settled into what on the outside among heterosexuals would have been common law marriages, which did not however quell interest in a young new arrival. Beating the older, and bigger, man down in fight marked Harsh as off limits to any further attention.

In another incident, deeper into his sentence, Harsh, by his own admission, killed another prisoner in self-defense with a knife when he sought return of precious bar of store-bought soap the other man had stolen. The investigation of the killing ground to a halt when no other prisoner owned to knowing any of the who or why that left the dead man on the ground. Violence and the potential for violence was the daily stuff of existence in the camp. In most other respects, however, life on the chain gang was a monotonous subsistence.[19]

Awakened at dawn six days a week by a guard clanging a piece of iron, the prisoners trooped to a breakfast inevitably of lumpy grits covered in a greasy, pasty gravy, a piece of fried sow belly, a pone of cornbread and a cup of chicory coffee. Lunch would be another pone of cornbread to go with field peas and boiled sow belly brought from the camp to wherever the gang was working and ladled out of a milk can. As likely as not, a prisoner could as easily find a boiled mouse in his scoop of peas as a piece of sow belly. Supper was more of the same. The only relief was food purchased from outside with the small amounts of money the prisoners could scrounge and jugs of corn liquor smuggled in by trusty prisoners with the guards connivance, five dollars a gallon, plus two dollars for the smuggler. In between these diversions there was exhausting, usually backbreaking work.[20]

Each man wore shackles around his ankles connected by a chain that had linked in the middle about a yard of another chain with a ring at the free end. This way, any number of men could be connected together to form the chained working crew. The work was mostly road work, cutting roadways through hills and filling other areas, calling for the wholesale moving of a lot of dirt mainly by picks and shovels and a few mule-drawn wagons. It was the hardest of work, especially in the dusty heat, work that a new man had to endure with blistered and bloodied hands until he formed the calluses of a veteran. Chained men have to function almost as a piece, and that drove the way the men worked. It was called "picking up the lick," a system in which the picks of those using them rose and fell in unison, as did shovels of others scoop and lift to the wagons as one. "The timing of the lick, the rhythm, the cadence that was invariably accompanied by a work chant – 'Pick'em up high-ER! Let'em fall hard-ER!' – made the whole proceeding like a shoddy ballet," Harsh recalled, "and this made us forget the deadening monotony of what we were doing."

Slackness could bring a man a flogging, even though flogging prisoners was by that time illegal. It was all, Harsh reflected years later, part of the plan. "The idea of rehabilitation had no place in the Georgia penal system of those days; punishment in the Old Testament sense was the only concept even remotely considered. If in the process the prisoner's spirit was broken and he was turned into a dead-eyed automaton, so much the better. It would make the guards' job easier."

The stoic Harsh made the best of it, in good part by taking to heart, he later wrote, the words of another prisoner: "What they do to us here in prison isn't really important; it's what we've done to ourselves ... what we allow to happen within us." Harsh was determined to survive, never abandoning hope that one day he would be free. How that came, even he probably could not have imagined.[21]

A bloody prison break in 1933 that left the chief guard of the cage camp dead, executed with his own gun by an escaping prisoner, led to a grand jury investigation of the incident and chain gang conditions in general. Harsh and nine other prisoners testified. One result was that all ten were transferred to Fulton County, whose county camp system, Harsh recollected, even then had a reputation among prisoners for humane, decent treatment, essentially being everything the cage camp hadn't been. After a few months Harsh was made a trusty and lost his leg irons. He recalled that day as one where his life became more than a matter of grim day to day routine and a struggle for survival. "I began to have more hope that my future life could have more meaning than the senseless giving of an eye for an eye."[22]

For the last five years he was jailed, Harsh was a hospital orderly, his evident education having early caught the eye of Dr. Paul McDonald, chief physician of the Fulton County penal system, who had examined Harsh after his transfer. "By any yardstick ... a great man," Harsh wrote of McDonald. "And I treasure the memory of my five years association and friendship with him."

It would prove to be one of the most fruitful and pivotal times of Harsh's life, and certainly the most crucial since his arrest, trial and sentencing. Among other things, the doctor opened his library to Harsh, who had managed to feed his lifelong voracious appetite for reading even in the cage camp. With a small room of his own in the hospital, Harsh had the privacy and time to work his way through McDonald's medical library. This he did in record time and with the comprehension of his fine mind.

He wrote of no time when he imagined how his medical studies might open the prison gate for him, but that would be the case. Harsh's reading gave another man his life and him his freedom.

It was a night in October 1940, when a cold rain turned into an ice storm that shut down the Atlanta area, closing roads and streets, bringing telephone and power lines to the ground. One of the last vehicles out was a prison system car bringing a sixty-one-year-old convict to the system hospital, where Harsh and another orderly, a black trusty, were on watch, a civilian records clerk and the deputy warden the only other souls around. The convict had a fever and pain and swelling in his right lower abdomen, classic appendicitis.

The patient needed transport to a hospital capable of handling the surgery. But the prison hospital phones were dead and no one was going anywhere on the iced over roads. The deputy warden, Max Tyree, put his finger on the problem and the only solution. "There ain't nobody goin' nowhere. …There ain't no phone … there ain't no lights … there ain't no power. George, you're on your own."

Harsh was incredulous. "You mean … you mean …I got to operate."

"I ain't said no such damn thing. I ain't said nothin' to you. In fact I ain't even seen you today," Harsh recalled Tyree saying, his real meaning plain.

There was no choice. Two lanterns, two flashlights and three candles lit the crude operating room Harsh set up. The air was heavy with ether the other orderly dripped on a mask over the patient's face and with the alcohol used to sterilize the instruments. Both Harsh and the orderly braced themselves with a stiff tumblerful of medicinal alcohol and ginger ale before Harsh made his incision. He removed the inflamed appendix, tied off the stump, and sutured the wound.

Harsh recollected he and the orderly capped the surgery with at least two tumblers each of alcohol and ginger ale, joined by the clerk and the deputy warden who had waited in the next room. The deputy warden, Harsh recalled, had chewed up three cigars during the surgery, mulling over how he could explain it all if the convict died on the table. It was two days before Paul McDonald could make it through the ice storm to the hospital and examine the patient, who made a full recovery.

"That was a good job you two did," Harsh recalled McDonald saying. "But George ... that incision. Good God ... you weren't doing a Caesarean on an elephant, you know."

McDonald followed up his tongue-in-cheek admonishment by writing a full report of the incident and sending it to the governor, accompanied by a personal letter. Other copies went to Harsh's attorney, William Howard. The machinery was set in motion for a full pardon. Harsh was paroled on November 21, 1940. By mid-January 1941, the governor announced pardons for both Harsh and the other orderly. Harsh had been jailed for taking a life, then Gov. Rivers said in his official statement, and now he had restored a life. Justice had been served.[22]

### Canadian Second Chance

"I roamed the streets of Atlanta like a fleshed out ghost," Harsh recalled of the six weeks after his release. Old friends and family were kind, but had no idea how to help him re-enter a world without guards. Though America wasn't yet in the European fighting, war plants were gearing up to support the effort, but Harsh figured his prison past would rule out any job for him. Just after his release, Harsh had declared his intention to study medicine and "spend the rest of my life in an effort to relieve human suffering," but there is no evidence he ever acted on that. The penal system had taught him no trades useful on the outside, no legal trades anyway. Some old prison associates looked him up and offered him a one-third interest in their numbers racket, seeking to trade on Harsh's reputation as a killer to encourage debt collections. Harsh was tempted, and that troubled him.[24]

He left Atlanta roaming, and landed in Montreal. He found a city on a war footing, doing its bit for the British Commonwealth, and the purposeful resolve he witnessed impressed him.

He also found Americans who had crossed the border to join the Canadian forces. One, a Tennessean named Chuck Leach, was also an ex-con. With his record, he'd faced the same problem as Harsh in the States, but the Canadian services needed men and weren't checking backgrounds too carefully. Leach was being sworn into the Royal

Canadian Air Force the next day and encouraged Harsh to join him. When Harsh came to the question on the form as to whether he had ever been convicted of a felony, Leach advised, "Just take a deep breath and put down a big, fat NO. It won't be the last time you'll have to lie in order to eat, y'know."

In his memoirs, Harsh reflected on his decision. "I was trying to prove to my own satisfaction that I really belonged in this world as a full member of the society that had once expelled me....There is nothing more dangerous in this world than a man who is trying to prove something...he is a mass of quavering self-doubts, and he will do anything, make any play to the grandstand, to still this uncertain voice he hears within himself."

Within days he was in the RCAF, headed for aerial gunnery training. His American citizenship, all rights so recently restored, was now forfeit, but he didn't see that as an immediate concern. "If I didn't come back from the war," he wrote, "well it just wasn't worth worrying about at the time."[25]

Harsh finished at the head of his class and was awarded a commission. He shipped out to England, eventually to be gunnery officer of the 102 Squadron, Bomber Command. He recorded the time as one when the terror of flying missions – when he would wryly muse on the artistic aesthetics of anti-aircraft fire – were balanced by the idyllic hours spent with his new comrades, including Chuck Leach. (Leach, a Spitfire pilot, would earn the Distinguished Flying Cross, personally awarded by King George VI.)

It was a time, Harsh remembered, when the war seemed to make all the normal things of life seem tenuous, a fact driven home by Leach's eventual death in combat, which Harsh made the occasion for a three-day drunk. But there were high points, such as the critical raid against German submarine pens for which 102 Squadron was seen off personally by Winston Churchill.

But there came a last mission, one that he was originally not even slated to fly. On the mission over Cologne on the night of October 5-6, 1942, his luck ran out. The bomber carrying him was bracketed by anti-aircraft fire and the crew had to bail out.

Severely injured in his parachute landing, Harsh recalled ironically the "good natured curiosity" he found in the German soldiers who took him prisoner, making sure to relieve him of his American cigarettes, and his hearing for the first time a phrase in heavily accented English he was to hear many times to come: "For you der var is ofer."

Interrogated and hospitalized, Harsh recuperated before he was transported to prison. He was regarded as a curiosity by German soldiers he and his guard encountered at train stations, so much so that he felt like an animal in a zoo. They tried out their English on him, and shared rations. "The zoo feeling left me entirely when they began breaking out flasks of schnapps, and before the trip was over I had learned the chorus of the Horst Wessel by heart." His last stop was Stalag Luft III.[26]

Stalag Luft III. This would be George Harsh's home for many months as he played his key role as enforcer of security measures surrounding the planned mass breakout since dubbed "The Great Escape".
(British Imperial War Museum)

The prison camp was a three hundred yards-square space enclosed by two fences about nine feet high and five feet apart, strung with barbed wire, the outer fence about thirty yards from the treeline. Between the fences were coils of barbed wire described by Harsh's fellow prisoner, writer Paul Brickhill as "so thickly in parts you could hardly see through it." Thirty feet inside the inner fence ran the deadline, a shin-high wire that guards could shoot a prisoner for crossing. Every 150 yards along the outer fence stood a "goon box," a watch tower manned around the clock. Wooden barracks were subdivided into eighteen rooms, each fifteen feet by fifteen feet, each intended to house eight men. Three other rooms, built for two men, were for higher ranking officers. The whole subdivided compound was intended to house about one thousand Allied air force officers, but during Harsh's time housed about six hundred. About one hundred miles southeast of Berlin, in a desolate area of Silesia, it was the acme of German prison camps, built by design on loose, sandy soil thought deadly for anyone tunneling. Harsh's first experience was a vetting, questioning on his unit and the conditions of his capture. It was how the prisoners guarded against the Germans slipping in a spy. Then he had to adjust to once again being in prison.[27]

"For me the psychological adjustment was basically a minor one. I had been through this before," Harsh recounted. Still, the irony of it all struck him squarely between the eyes. He hadn't quite, in his mind, adjusted to the idea of being a free man before he once again found himself in a prison. "If the gods considered this a joke, I took a bloody pale view of their sense of humor." Nevertheless, he soon slipped back into the old routine from the chain gang of living one day at a time. There was now, though, a camaraderie and esprit de corps among the prisoners of war that there hadn't been in the cage camp. And of course, there was the X Organization.[28]

Roger Bushell had arrived in Stalag Luft III at about the same time as Harsh. Born in South Africa, Bushell had been a first class barrister in London before the war. A squadron leader, he had been a prisoner most of the time since late May 1940. "A big, tempestuous man with broad shoulders and the most chilling pale-blue eyes I ever saw," in the description of Paul Brickhill, he sported a scar in the corner of his right eye – a relic of his youthful days as an Olympic skier – that gave a droop to this eye that, to Brickhill, made him look brooding and sinister. A veteran of three escape attempts, he had once gotten within a few feet of the Swiss border before being recaptured. His treatment at the hands of the Gestapo after his last failed escape before being thrown into Stalag Luft III had left him with a deep hatred of his captors that went beyond that for a mere enemy. He was Big X, the chief of the X Organization.[29]

It was about seven months after Harsh's arrival when the X Organization brought him into the inner circle. On a walk around the compound perimeter Wally Flood told him of the plan for the three tunnels, nicknamed Tom, Dick and Harry, that would each go down thirty feet before turning horizontal. Through them, Bushell hoped to take out most, perhaps all, of the prisoners in a mass escape that, even if most were recaptured, would tie up German resources for perhaps months. 'He's determined to create as big a flap as possible right here in the middle of Germany," said Floody. How, Harsh asked, could they ever hope to keep from the Germans an effort of the size needed to carry that plan off. That, said a smiling Floody, was Harsh's job.

Floody and Harsh had met on Harsh's second day in the camp, and the Canadian mining engineer turned Spitfire pilot had become a fast friend, a friendship that would endure until the end of Harsh's life. Floody was the only person in the camp to whom Harsh had confided his whole story. Floody's mining engineer background meant that he was the natural tunneler, but he knew he wanted Harsh topside for him. He hadn't told Bushell his reasons, but he told Harsh: it was Harsh's prison history. "I told Roger that that if I was going to spend the next year or so of my life prowling around down in the bowels of Germany I wanted a man topside, protecting me, in whom I could feel some trust,"[30]

Harsh was to select two hundred men for his security force. The task was to set up a clandestine system for watching the "ferrets," those Germans who prowled the compound by day, walking at random through barracks, looking under the barracks and generally looking for any sign whatsoever of an escape attempt brewing. More than just the tunnels needed protection, though. The scale of the breakout operation envisioned fostered a covert mammoth covert industrial complex in the camp that turned out everything needed to escape, ranging from the tools for digging to forged identification papers and travel documents, civilian-looking clothing, reproduced maps and even crude but useful compasses. To guard it all from prying eyes, Harsh and his helpers looked for patterns in the ferrets' movements and surprise checks and set up a system of mobile and stationary watchers to keep tabs on every German who entered the compound. A silent communication system of safety and danger signals – "the way a certain garment was hanging on a clothes line, the manner in which an empty Red Cross carton was placed on an incinerator. The way in which a certain door had been left ajar" – allowed warnings to be transmitted from one side of the camp to the other at almost the speed of a shout.

There were times, however, when emergency steps had to be improvised. On one occasion a ferret darted into the barrack where the entrance to Tom was open. The entrance minder had seven seconds warning and the scramble began. The ferret was three paces from the room where the tunnel entrance opened when a door to a side room opened and Harsh came barreling out, crashing into the ferret, sending both sprawling on the floor. Prisoners crowded around and helped both to their feet, Harsh wincing in pain, holding his knee and apologizing to the guard for his clumsiness. Befuddled, the guard brushed himself off and, with a grim smile, walked out. The prisoners in the next room had enough time to close and hide the tunnel entrance. They complimented Harsh on his timing. "George was swearing too much to listen," wrote Paul Brickhill. "He really had hurt his knee."[31]

This played out for over a year, during which the Germans discovered one tunnel and the prisoners decided to close down another. But in March 1944, Harry was judged complete. The escape was set for the night of March 24, the dark of the moon. The climax of the months of planning is one of the great tragedies of escape lore: Harry was at least ten feet too short, the opening out in a clear area instead of inside the woods, as planned.

Only seventy-six men got out before the escape was discovered. Only three made it to safety. The rest were recaptured after a manhunt that covered Germany and engaged thousands of troops and police. Fifty were shot, including Bushell. Many of the dead men Harsh had become close to. "When the Gestapo murdered them, something within me died also," Harsh wrote over forty years later. "I am not trying to be dramatic." The whole concept the escape, which he thought too risky at the time, he later came to view as "an act of military madness, a futile empty gesture and the needless sacrifice of fifty lives."[32]

He and Floody had not made it out, but were considered by the Germans as prime suspects in the conspiracy. They were among twenty-five prisoners singled out to be sent to a punishment camp over twenty miles away. There they remained through the last winter of the war, when the advance of the Russian Army forced the camp's evacuation. The prisoners were forced on a march west, a trek in which they quickly became mixed with a horde of refugees. In late March 1945, Harsh, Floody and about one hundred other prisoners were liberated by Russian troops.[33]

### The Last Miles ...

After the war, Harsh worked at a number of jobs, and also married, living mainly in New York and New Jersey. In 1971 he published his memoir, *Lonesome Road*. He had already written a foreword to Paul Brickhill's *The Great Escape* and on the heels of the 1963 movie based on Brickhill's book this "wild, wild, rambunctious soul," as Brickhill had described him, was enjoying some renown for being a participant in the famous breakout. In 1972, he published an op-ed in the New York Times opposing capital punishment, using his own case as evidence that wealth could prevent a convicted murderer from being executed where someone not wealthy would die. It was an argument almost verbatim of that he had also made in his memoir: "With sufficient money, a capital case can be kept in the courts until the defendant dies of old age. You can't hang a million dollars. ...This is not cynicism: It is truth. And I am living proof."[34]

Harsh reportedly tried to commit suicide on Christmas Eve of 1974, but that was never conclusively substantiated. Nevertheless, he was by other accounts dogged by fits of depression in those years. After what was reported as a stroke he went to live with Wally Flood in Toronto. He died on Jan. 25, 1980.

He was praised by some after his death as a hero, but he himself, reflecting in his memoirs, had had the last word. Looking back at the key event that had shaped his life, the spree of robbing and killing, he had written "Even to this day I have a hard time explaining it satisfactorily, even to myself." For Harsh, it colored everything that followed and for the extraordinary events that came shortly before his release and afterward he gave himself no real praise. He doesn't even mention in his memoirs that while in the prison he was credited with saving seventy men locked in a building that caught fire. He labeled nothing he ever did as heroic. The real hero, he wrote " is the quiet man who goes about the daily task of just living ... who just carries out the routine, often boring, processes of his daily life without fanfare and yet, through it all, stays reasonably cheerful and brings a share of happiness to those who love and depend on him. To me this quiet man is the real unsung hero of the human epic. And his is the type of courage I lack."[35]

Airman Harsh (British Imperial War Museum)

George Harsh in the early 1970s, with most of a hard life behind. He claimed near the end, to lack the courage to be "a quiet man" who lived an honorable if ordinary life, a true hero in Harsh's eyes.

# 8

# Up From Slave Row – The Making of William Henry Heard

William H. Heard, circa 1885

In the man from Augusta the young William Henry Heard saw a glimpse of what he could become. The sights and sounds of the occasion, the awe and wonder of the moment stuck with him the rest of his days.

By Heard's later reckoning, it was early 1867 when the Rev. William Jefferson White came speak in Heard's hometown of Elberton. White, the son of a white father and a mixed black and Creek mother, was a Baptist minister in Augusta and an educator working with the Georgia division of the Freedmen's Bureau, the agency tasked with helping the former slaves cope with the travails of their new freedom in the Reconstruction South. He was the Bureau-appointed apostle ministering on the need for the freedmen to found and support schools, insist on fair labor contract terms from white landowners (often their former masters), and generally learn to depend on themselves.[1]

In time the man from Augusta and his admirer would become friends. "He was the first colored man I had ever seen who was well educated, and who could use the King's English readily, accurately and convincingly," Heard wrote years later on the deep impression White had made. "I was determined from that night to be a man, and to fill an important place in life's arena."[2]

Heard was in his early seventies when he recalled this moment when the compass needle of his life trembled and swung onto a course he hoped to follow. He was not quite seventeen when he made White's acquaintance, but for only a little over eighteen months had he been free. He knew little then of the world beyond Elbert County. He had probably yet to have ever left the county's boundaries, even though by early 1867 he had gained a rudimentary education and had been working some months as a school teacher for black children. That marked him already with some distinction for a young freedman, but White had given him a glimpse of the larger world. At least from that moment, though, he had an idea of what he wanted to do in life, if only the vaguest of notions, filled less with hopes and plans than with the uncertain and the unknowable.

"To fill an important place in life's arena" was a tall order for a young freedman on the cusp of adulthood in the South where the sounds of battle had barely echoed away. But the elderly man writing in the early 1920s of his first meeting with White looked back across nearly six decades of a life that included rising to a bishopric in the African Methodist Episcopal Church and serving as American diplomat and missionary to Liberia.

He could – and did, and not without a good deal of justification – let a few wisps of pride seep into his sparse and generally self-effacing memoir. The stamp of the time and place of his upbringing in the upper Savannah River valley is there, too, and deep if seldom remembered with any fondness.

What was hinted at, though, was a certain pride in having met the challenges his early years had thrown at him, overcoming them, and venturing on to a life he could not have imagined on that night in Elberton. That upbringing was the crucible that had produced his steel.

## Slave Row

William Henry Heard was born "in corn plowing time" of 1850 (on June 25, as near as he could later reckon) on the plantation of Thomas Jones in the Longstreet community of Elbert County, about ten miles east of Elberton, the county seat. His mother, Parthenia, was a "breeder," as he later recalled, a slave woman who had children regularly and was given work in the fields near enough the slave quarters so that she could nurse and care for her children. She would bear five children by the time she died of typhoid fever in 1859, when William was nine and his youngest brother, George, was only five weeks. Heard's earliest memories centered around the cabin his mother was given on the Jones plantation, a simple one-room cabin of pine logs with a puncheon floor. In the winter the cracks between the logs were daubed and chinked with mud to keep out the cold. In the summer, the chinking was knocked out so what breezes blew would keep the cabin cool. The price for that luxury, though, was frogs, lizards and snakes as household guests. "At night you were just as likely to find a snake curled up in your bed taking his rest as you were to take your rest," Heard recalled.[3]

His father was George Heard, a blacksmith and wheelwright on a neighboring plantation about three miles from the Jones farm. He was owned by Thomas Jefferson Heard, one of the sons of Stephen Heard, considered one of Georgia's governors during the revolutionary period and regarded as a local hero in Elbert County (although his most legendary deed – an escape from a British prison in Augusta on the eve of his hanging with the help of a slave woman – is probably just a fanciful myth). Thomas Heard, according to William's account (which was no doubt passed down from his father) was also George Heard's father.[4]

Such a blood relationship between master and slave in the antebellum South would not have been uncommon, but also rarely acknowledged openly. The 1870 Census list for Elbert County does list George Heard, then fifty-seven years old, as a mulatto, and details from William Heard's memoir provide some clues that the claim of George Heard's paternity could well be true and at least tacitly owned to by members of the Heard family. George Heard was able to visit his children's mother twice a week, usually once on Wednesday nights and again on Saturday nights, with a standing pass to be away from the Heard plantation until the following Monday morning. (William Heard does not mention whether his parents were ever able to actually marry, even in the unofficial way slaves were allowed.) Such passes for slaves weren't unusual in similar circumstances, but the regular visitation arrangement would seem to indicate that George Heard was regarded with some exceptional level of trust or favoritism by Thomas Heard. It is not necessarily, though, a tacit acknowledgement that George Heard carried his blood. But other facts may rise to circumstantial evidence.

At least by mid-1865, almost immediately after the end of the war, according to his son's recollections, George Heard had established a blacksmithing and wheelwright shop on the outskirts of Elberton, on a main road from Washington, to the south in Wilkes County. That a newly freed slave could do that so early after the war and before the efforts of the Freedman's Bureau took hold in earnest in Elbert County could well indicate that the hand of the Heard family played a role. Perhaps directly, with tools or money, or perhaps at least that George Heard had been allowed, as some favored slaves were, especially mechanics and craftsmen, to work for pay off the plantation and accumulate the small cache of hard money that allowed him the tools and whatever building sheltered his trade. The practice of slaves hiring out had been restricted during the war, but nevertheless took place. All told, it seems safe ground to say that George Heard held a favored position among Thomas Heard's slaves, which may have served as as much tacit acknowledgment of the blood kinship claimed as Thomas Heard desired to show. There would be still another possible unspoken acknowledgement to come, this time not to George but to William as he moved toward young manhood.

William Heard recounted his childhood in only seven scant paragraphs of his memoirs, laying out only the basic facts. In the 1930s a program of the federal Work Projects Administration paid writers to record for posterity the recollections of still living former slaves. It wasn't uncommon for them to recall some times from their childhoods as happy, at least happy from their perspective in their eighties or so. Heard recorded nothing of any such happier times himself, though it would seem certain there must have been at least some lighter moments. For whatever reasons of his own, however, he apparently did not see fit to make them part of his life story. Instead, what stuck foremost in his mind as he set down his account were the two times before he was ten that he, his mother, and his siblings had been sold.

The first time he may have remembered only vaguely, only that it happened, as it took place when he was about five. His mother and the three children she had at the time, including William, were sold as part of an estate. The buyer, Lindsey Smith, owned a plantation in the Flatwoods community of Elbert County, only a few miles away from the plantation of Thomas Jones. By all indications, William's father was able to continue seeing his family, which continued to grow. In 1857, after about two years on the Smith plantation, William's mother and all her children – four by then – were bought by John Trenchard, founder and headmaster of the Elberton Academy, a preparatory school in the county seat. After years of working the fields between bearing and caring for children, William's mother was to be a cook for the boarding house Trenchard kept to house his students who came from some distance away.[5]

"Professor Trenchard was an Iowa man, and what we considered a fair master," Heard remembered. But William's time in the new surroundings turned out to be short. In 1859, typhoid fever claimed both his mother and his oldest sister, leaving him the oldest of the remaining four children, the youngest five-week-old George. William was sent to plow on a farm and the other children were dispersed to other black families. William would spend over five years as a field hand, the whole of the war years. He didn't later recollect the precise date when he made himself free but did recall that it was about four weeks after he had seen a troop of blue-coated cavalry pass in the distance as he plowed. If we trust this vague recollection by Heard, his sighting of Union cavalry would have most likely occurred in May 1865 as Union forces fanned out across northeast Georgia in pursuit of Confederate president Jefferson Davis or such wanted Confederates as Wilkes County's Robert Toombs. In any case, his break to emancipation most likely occurred after the collapse of the Confederacy meant he was already free. On his last day as a slave, he and others were stacking when the overseer, drunk, decided to beat them all. "That night I took all my belongings, put them in a pocket handkerchief and 'went to freedom.' Thus ended slavery with me."[6]

He went to live with his father, who by this time had already established his blacksmith and wheelwright shop near Elberton, not too far, Heard recalled, from an elementary school.[7] There were no established schools for blacks yet in Elbert County in that summer of 1865, the program of Freedmen's Bureau tasked with establishing schools still being in its infancy. And in fact the Bureau's efforts to start black schools was always less involved with direct aid than it was dependent on Northern philanthropy and the encouraging the freedmen themselves to found and contribute to the schools' support as part of encouraging self-sufficiency. Hence, one of the reasons that William White had made his fateful visit to Elberton in 1867.

There had been no legal way for a slave to be educated during William's childhood, though some illegal schools for slaves had existed. William White, in fact, had organized several in the Augusta area before the war. The question of educating blacks had been a point of considerable debate among both those white Southerners who hoped to see slavery eventually ended and those dedicated to preserving it. Reformers, led mainly by Methodist, Baptist and Episcopal ministers, had pushed a bill in the Georgia legislature in early 1865 to overturn the state law against teaching slaves to read and write. The State Senate was about evenly divided on the bill but it failed to gain real support in the House.[8]

But the fifteen-year-old newly freed William already had enough of a taste to know what he lacked and what he wanted. Throughout the war years, his years as a plow hand, he had attended a Sunday school for black children at the Methodist Episcopal Church in Elberton. "In this Sunday school we were taught the Bible and Catechism, and committed much to memory by having the same repeated to us in the Sunday school, and then some member of the white family carried this out during the week; so that there were those of us who could repeat whole Psalms and chapter after chapter in the Shorter Catechism," Heard recalled. He had not been taught to read and write, though, and this he now set out to change. His father, who himself never learned to read or write, paid a white youth ten cents a lesson to teach William what the youth had learned at the school almost in sight of the blacksmith shop, using a Webster's Blue Back Spelling Book. 'I studied spelling, reading, and arithmetic all in this one book.'"[9]

Toward the end of 1865, young William, then without any last name that he ever mentioned (and maybe not even then using the name William, a point on which he is never clear), went to work for "a farmer named William Henry Heard, from whom I received my name." By their contract, the youth was paid five dollars a month and received a nightly school lesson from Heard. It was a fair bargain in times when the Georgia Freedman's Bureau guidelines, in place since June 1865, specified pay of at least seven dollars a month for an adult freedman field hand. This is another case where the elderly bishop's memoir, sparse with details in places, seems as telling in what it doesn't relate as in what it does. Heard noted his father's supposed parentage almost in passing and doesn't mention it again. He neglects entirely to mention – though it seems highly unlikely he would not have known – that the William Henry Heard who hired him and whose last name he took as his own was Thomas Jefferson Heard's son, a man probably his uncle, who perhaps felt some sense of obligation of his own to give the young William a job and schooling. And of all the people he had encountered so far in his few years, why take Heard's name as his own instead of, say, the kindly remembered Trenchard? William's explicit statement of taking his name from William Henry Heard makes it clear he didn't simply assume the last name his father had taken from his owner and own purported father. In any case, William Heard's memoir with its claim in print of possible kinship to one of the oldest first families of Elbert County appeared in 1924, and so far as is known, no Heard descendant (which includes this writer) has seen cause to dispute it.[10]

The work on the Heard plantation was "from can to cain't," from sunup till dark, but the work of the day for the young William still wasn't finished when the sun went down. Only then did what he regarded as his most important work begin. He went to the main house, waited till his uncle had finished his supper and gave his recitation of his day's lesson. The field hands were given an hour at midday to eat and to feed their livestock, and some took the opportunity of any leftover time to grab extra sleep. William did not. He used the time to get his day's lesson down. His clothes had no pockets, he recalled later, so he removed the coverboards from his lesson book and carried the rolled book under his cap, much to the amusement of some of those with whom he worked. This relationship with his uncle lasted at least until early June 1866, until his uncle's crop was "laid by," that time of respite from daily toil in the fields of young, vulnerable crops. William then went to live again with his father.[11]

### Teacher

William worked in his father's shop in the mornings and late afternoons and, for six weeks, during the heart of the day attended a small newly established school for blacks. "I studied spelling, reading, writing, arithmetic, and geography. At the end of this time I could spell words of five or six syllables, compose, and write a letter and understood the four rules of arithmetic: addition, subtraction, multiplication, and division." At the end of that month and a half, and after some private lessons, he took an examination to become a teacher himself. That fall, he and an assistant taught at another black school that had been established in Elberton with the help of the Freedmen's Bureau. He was paid by the children's' parents, one dollar per month per pupil for the term. With over one hundred students, at the end of the three-month term he had over three hundred dollars. "That was big money in those days, and it gave me a start in the world of economics," the elderly bishop reflected.

He was also continuing with his own education. From a teacher at the white school, James Lofton, he took additional lessons in grammar, mathematics and history. "I saw opening up along the intellectual horizon things I never dreamed of," Heard recalled. "I was a man of good memory, they said, and I got much from my studies, so that I went on teaching and in the second year I received a second grade certificate, taught the public school and was rewarded as before."[12]

What he saw going on around him in his corner of the Reconstruction South, though, was also pulling him in another direction. He had never before given thought to politics, but now he did. The lure of politics, or rather the realization that some involvement in politics was essential for freedmen, led him indirectly to his first connection with the AME Church. In early 1867, probably shortly after his meeting William White, Heard ventured to Augusta, where he heard a speech delivered by Henry McNeal Turner, also a minister, but also a political organizer and firebrand for the cause of the freedmen. Like the meeting with White, Heard's meeting Turner was fateful.

Turner had been born in Newberry, South Carolina, in 1834, but unlike Heard, he had never been a slave. Like, Heard, however, he was of mixed race. Turner's paternal grandmother had been, according to family accounts, a white plantation owner; his paternal grandfather, an African brought to the United States but not sold into slavery, instead ending up with a Quaker family. Turner had gained an education while working as a general errand boy in the office of a firm of attorneys in Abbeville, S.C., and had felt a call to the Methodist ministry. In the antebellum years, he had traveled the South as an itinerant evangelist before entering the ministry of the AME Church in 1858, ending up in Washington D.C.

During the war he served as a chaplain with the 1st U.S. Colored Troops. After the war he returned to evangelizing in the South, mostly in Georgia. By 1867, though, he was fully immersed in politics, working to organize the Georgia Republican Party. At the same time, Turner also became active in the movement encouraging the freedmen to emigrate to Africa.[13] Between 1865 and 1877, the most active years of the movement in the state, nearly 1,000 blacks would move from Georgia to Liberia, nearly a third of all the newly free who made the voyage in those years.[14] That movement, too, would play a part in William Heard's future. The Turner speech that Heard attended, "The Negro in All Ages," limned some of the thoughts of this developing movement, and in Heard fanned to flame the desire to become more involved. "My life," the elderly bishop wrote, "is largely what it is because of the impressions of that meeting."[15]

Back in Elberton, William became a secretary of the local "Colored Methodist Episcopal Church," as he referred to it.[16] And he also for the first time became involved in politics, because certainly with Turner's sermons and likely also with White's, what he was hearing was wrapped in the words of scripture but it had at least an undertone of political action. This would have been a difficult undertaking if he hadn't had the fortune to attract the attention of an Elberton resident who had become probably the most hated man in the county, Amos Akerman.

Unlike the encounter with William White or Henry Turner, Heard doesn't note the details of his and Akerman's first meeting in his memoir – he even mistakenly gives his first name as James – saying only that Akerman played a crucial role in his future. Akerman would prove to be a dangerous man to know and the politics William Heard now became involved in, a dangerous business.[17]

The time and place in which Amos Tappan Akerman lived and worked during his most active years stamps him as an unusual and intriguing character. Born in New Hampshire and graduating from Dartmouth College in 1842, Ackerman had forayed into the South in search of teaching positions, first as a headmaster at a school in North Carolina and later as a tutor in Savannah. He gained admission to the Georgia bar in 1850, and by the late years of that decade he was well established as an attorney in Elberton. He also acquired substantial acres and enough slaves to work them.

When the threat of secession arose in 1860 following the election of Abraham Lincoln to the presidency, Akerman had been quick to join the fight to stay in the union, among other things becoming a founding member of the Constitutional Union Club in nearby Athens, the key political and cultural hub of Georgia's northeast corner. The war years, though, found him at least for a time serving with the Georgia state troops, including one stint in a state cavalry unit. After the war, Akerman joined the Republican Party and became active in aiding the Freedmen's Bureau. Neither action made him especially popular in Elbert County.[18]

It became part of the tradition in Elbert County in the years after Reconstruction that the county, essentially untouched by the war until the very last days, was bypassed by much of the Reconstruction turmoil because it had no railroad link. John McIntosh, in his 1940 history of Elbert County, trumpets that legacy and notes that Elberton never had an established office of the Freedman's Bureau. That is apparently true. The rest of the local tradition, according to McIntosh, is that the county's resistance to Reconstruction was so virulent that it was immune to any of the entreaties or coercion by either the Freedman's Bureau or the supporting occupying federal forces that other counties such as Wilkes to the immediate south experienced. Thus, there was never any of the troubles in Elbert County experienced in other parts of the state, even in adjoining counties. That is not true.

As early as January 1866, federal troops occupied the county at the request of the Freedman's Bureau when bureau agents found that local land owners were making labor contracts with former slaves for sometimes as little as two dollars a month, less than a third the wages set in the Bureau's guidelines. This led one of Elbert County's more prominent planters and political forces of the immediate postwar era, William H. Mattox, to write a letter to Governor Charles Jenkins protesting that the Bureau's set wages were too high for the county and were an unfair burden and expectation in a county where the people, "as reliable & honest as any in God's creation," were already for the most part paying their hands one-third of the crop plus their maintenance. Mattox, a former Confederate officer, had resigned his commission in early 1862 to return home to Elbert County, where he had spent the war years mainly profiteering and using the proceeds to acquire substantially more acres and a number of gristmills. After the war he parlayed his position in the county to become active in Democratic politics and eventually would be elected to the legislature. He's worth so much mention in William Heard's story because he was also, by marriage, a relative of Heard's, as Mattox's wife was a niece of Thomas Jefferson Heard. In the end the Freedman's Bureau got its way. By February 1866 the major commanding the federal forces in Elbert County reported that "a majority of the planters are sufficiently persuaded to make honest contracts with the freedmen."[19]

The elections of 1866, before William entered the political fray, give a glimpse of the arena. The November 6 edition of the *Elberton Gazette* described what was probably Akerman's first attempt to organize the freedmen's votes on behalf of the Republican Party. Federal troops were also on hand on voting day, headquartered just off the square. Akerman spoke for a reported two hours to a crowd of freedmen gathered in front of the federal troops' temporary headquarters, "haranguing them with great vehemence … with much effort to influence the minds of his dusky audience, no doubt with the intention of provoking 'a fat outrage'." At the end of his speech, Akerman distributed the voting tickets, formed the crowd into a column of two ranks and marched at the head of the column to the polls, under the eyes of the rest of the townspeople. "On entering the square, the ranks began to dissolve; one by one, and two by two, the Negroes fell out and went to white men and got {Democrat} tickets and went up and voted like honest men." Akerman, by the newspaper's account, was all alone by the time he reached the voting box and asked the county sheriff for protection while he voted.[20]

**Politics**

By 1872, Heard was chairman of the county Republican Party, but without Akerman directly at hand. The adopted Elbert Countian had moved on by then, serving from 1870 until into 1871 as U.S. Attorney General in the administration of President Ulysses S. Grant, where he led the fight against the rising of the Ku Klux Klan. In the election of 1872, Heard was a candidate for the state legislature on the Republican ticket, but lost. He blamed his defeat on the hijacking of the printed Republican voting tickets shipped to the Elberton post office. He and his assistant chairman, who could neither read nor write, were unable in the few hours they had produce enough handwritten tickets for all the precincts.[21]

Whether because of such or not – Heard gives no reasons except the lure of opportunity – by 1873, Heard was ready to leave Elbert County. In January of that year he took a teaching job in Mt. Carmel, South Carolina, in Abbeville County, just across the Savannah River from Elbert County. It was a six-months-a-year school, and he would earn forty dollars a month. He was nearly twenty-three, and it was the first time he had ever been out of Georgia.

He would teach in Abbeville County for four years, ands was able to continue his own studies with the help of the teacher of the local white school, concentrating on mathematics and Latin. He applied for one of five scholarships to the University of South Carolina that Abbeville County was allotted, the seats decided on a competitive basis. Heard won a scholarship and entered the classics department.[22]

He would not finish, however, being turned out of the university in 1877 when Reconstruction ended owing in good part to the deal struck by Southern Democrats following the sharply divided presidential election of 1876. In return for Southern Democrats supporting the candidacy of Republican Rutherford B. Hayes, who had lost the popular vote to the northern Democrat Samuel Tilden, the federal occupation of the South would end and the state governments would be returned to popular control. To Heard, the result of it all was a series of hard personal blows. Not only did he lose his place in the university, but he also lost his seat in the South Carolina legislature, won in the election of 1876. Before any of that, however,, he had also come close to losing his life.

Already a local organizer for the Republican Party, Heard had been appointed a deputy U.S. marshal with a responsibility to help keep order at the polls in the 1876 election. Local Democrats, however, managed to capture the tabulations of the results. When Heard tried to collect affidavits of the results he was captured, hogtied and taken across the river to Elbert County, ending up after two days at the Ruckersville community farm owned by the father of a man, Ed Starke, whom Heard believed to have been involved in the hijacking of the Republican voting tickets from the Elberton post office during the election of 1872. The men intended to kill him, and wanted Ed Starke to do it, but the idea was vetoed by Starke's father, whom Heard remembered as declaring, "There can be no killing on my place." That night, his captors took him to the Broad River, dividing Elbert County from Wilkes County to the south, and put him across. He walked to the county seat of Washington, took a train to Augusta using money he had kept secreted about him, crossed into South Carolina and made his way to Columbia, where he made an affidavit of his Abbeville County precinct results.[23]

The final blow to fall on Heard came when he was denied a chance to continue teaching in South Carolina. Clearly, what seemed a golden opportunity when he had looked beyond the world of Elbert County now held no prospects for him at all. He returned to Georgia but not to Elbert County, settling instead in Athens. He founded a school at a local AME church, Pierce Chapel, where he taught for nearly four years. He also studied law under the tutorship of a local attorney and in 1879 became co-publisher and editor of the *Athens Blade*, a newspaper aimed at a black readership. Aside from newspaper editorials, politics would mostly take a backseat during his time in Athens, though he did take part in the campaign for an independent Democrat, Congressman Emory Speare.

That toe-dipping into politics would, by way of patronage, earn him a plum appointment in 1880 as a railway postal clerk, working the lines from Atlanta to Macon and from Atlanta to Charlotte, North Carolina. But all the time there was a struggle going on inside him that, when he resolved it, would gather together all the influences and experiences he had had, and bring them into a sharper focus.[24]

**Preacher**

Heard nowhere in his recollections makes clear that his mentors William White and Henry McNeal Turner both being ministers played any role in his ultimate decision to turn to the church, but examined from a distance, their influence on his decision seems clear enough. Looking backwards, every path he took along the way seems to have met at the common point he arrived at in 1879. His final struggle to join the church, though, a struggle purely with himself instead of the outside world, was one as hard as any he had faced.

The spring of 1879 a "protracted meeting," as he later called it, of the AME Church opened in Athens. He went one evening. He ended up going every night for five weeks.

"One night before the services began, I reached the conclusion that open confession of my sins and acknowledgement of Christ as My Saviour was the thing to do. But I lacked Faith to do this, because I had felt nothing to assure me that I was saved," Heard wrote of the time. "So I carried out the idea by getting up in [sic] seat and undertaking to make this confession and acknowledgement.

"After some time standing on my feet, being unable to speak, FAITH CAME, my mouth flew open and I shouted for joy, and then I openly acknowledged that I was a sinner and that Christ was my Saviour, and that I was willing and ready to surrender ALL to Him."[25]

In what is otherwise a memoir written in steady, workmanlike prose, Heard's writing of this moment on the evening of May 16, 1879, has energy and emotion that is missing even from his recounting of his days as a slave or his steps toward an education. The measure of the moment is that it ended one struggle for him but opened another, this struggle one that he resolved quickly. He decided to abandon teaching and any plans for the law and become a minister. In June 1879 he applied and was approved to be an "exhorter," the necessary first step on his new road. He couldn't yet preach but he could read Bible passages before groups and discuss his interpretations. After three months of this before whatever gatherings he was asked to address, he preached a trial sermon before an examining board. He spoke for six minutes and earned a license as a local preacher, the lowest rung of the AME Church's ministry. Three months later, be was licensed as a traveling preacher.

In 1882, he was given a congregation in Aiken, S.C. Most of his preaching till then had been at missions around Atlanta, because he was still working as a railroad postal clerk. This job he now resigned, leaving a situation that paid him nearly $1,200 a year for one that paid less than $400. Except for his future diplomatic post, he would never again hold a job outside the church. Earlier the same year he had also become a husband, marrying Salisbury, North Carolina, native Josephine Henderson in Athens on January 21.[26]

The freshly minted pastor rose steadily in the church through a succession of congregations – Aiken and Charleston in South Carolina; Philadelphia; Baltimore; New York City; Boston; then back to Pennsylvania, with some additional duties in Delaware. Each congregation, he reported in his memoir with unconcealed satisfaction, he left larger and more financially sound than he found it.[27]

His path had taken him long ways from Georgia, but on at least one occasion he took an interest in matters in his home state, in a case that would bring his name to prominence in, mostly, Northern newspapers. In 1887, he was part of an unsuccessful legal action against the Georgia Railroad Company over its practice of charging black passengers full fare for separate accommodations that were judged less spacious and generally inferior to those in which whites traveled.[28]

Though he had sought no political office since 1876, he had clearly lost interest in neither politics, nor the law, nor the cause of reform. Nor had he lost touch with Henry McNeal Turner and Turner's interest in Liberia.

Turner, by now a bishop, had become a zealot in promoting black emigration to Liberia through his own International Migration Society, the earlier formed American Colonization Society and various similar organizations all with the same goal: Moving former slaves or their progeny out of the United States to the Eden they believed Africa to be. Turner himself traveled to Liberia for the first time only in 1891, combining missionary work with politics, meeting and becoming friends with many Liberian officials, among them Gen. R.A. Sherman, a Savannah, Georgia-born Liberian of mixed race who commanded the Liberian armed forces. It seems a measure of the influence he gained that the Liberians came to regard Turner as an informal diplomatic envoy. And through him they made known one of their peeves: American diplomats sent to Liberia seemed, more often than not, officious, condescending fools.

"The leading men, or a large number of them in Liberia, are disgusted with a majority of the representatives that our government sends over here," Turner wrote back to the editor of an AME Church newspaper in December 1891. "They say if our government cannot find sober, coolheaded, dignified and intelligent representatives of our own color to send here, ask the president to send white men." But Turner had someone else in mind. It took a while to work his will, over three years, but in February 1895 President Grover Cleveland appointed William Henry Heard as the American minister resident and consul general to Liberia.[29]

Heard accepted the diplomatic posting only on the condition that he could transfer to the Liberian conference of his church and carry out missionary work. This would not prove an obstacle, and he sailed for Africa, by way of England. London enthralled him. St. Paul's Cathedral, he was to write, was the "greatest church in the world" and the wonders of the British Museum, the attic of Great Britain's far-flung empire, was his first glimpse of the relics of times and places he had only read about. In years to come, on future trips to Europe, always en route to Africa, he would travel through France, Germany, Italy and Switzerland, but about none of these travels would he record awe and delight like this first experience wandering through the city that was the heart of the mighty British Empire. After a few days, however, he sailed from Liverpool with Turner, bound for Liberia, with a first stop in Sierra Leone his first chance to set foot on the African continent. It was an experience unlike any other for Heard.[30]

"We 'American Daddies' were welcomed by the natives. They followed us by the hundreds and rejoiced at our coming." That was the beginning of a few days of meeting with other missionary ministers and being feted by government officials who were already acquaintances of Turner. It was an overture to what would be repeated when Heard and Turner moved on to Liberia, 240 miles south and twenty-six hours away by ship.[31]

Heard stayed four years in Liberia, with at least one trip back to America during the period. When he returned, his wife returned with him. Diplomatic affairs seemed to take up little of his time – their recounting took up none of his memoirs – and he spent his time preaching and building a church in the Liberian capital, Monrovia, funded mostly by the Liberian government, together with some of his and Turner's own funds. The Eliza Turner Memorial Chapel, named for Turner's first wife, was the first AME church in Monrovia and as of this writing is still a vital and thriving church.

Heard and his wife returned to the United States in 1899, where he resumed the itinerant life of an AME minister, first back in Philadelphia, then variously in New York and back to Pennsylvania with even a stint in Atlanta. In 1908, he was elected a bishop. This ended his years as an itinerant minister, but not his travels. His bishopric was West Africa. In January 1909, he and his wife once again sailed for Liberia, this time with eight missionaries. He would be there for nearly eight years, called home by the church only when it seemed that the United States would be drawn into the world war that was already touching parts of Africa.[32]

A succession of posts for the bishop followed these years in Africa before Heard finally settled in Philadelphia, a city he had grown to love. He died there on September 12, 1937, and his death was reported worldwide. In his reflections during his last years there is little that could be called self-aggrandizement, though perhaps a little more credit to himself for his successes might well have been in order and be easily forgiven. He had, after all, come a long way from that slave cabin in Elbert County where mice, frogs and snakes vied with him for bed space. But what there is instead is an awe and sense of adventure that must hearken back to the seventeen-year-old seeing and listening to a man whom he wanted to be like, with no idea then how that might come to be.

The closest Heard ever comes to writing anything that could be his epitaph speaks to that: "I go forth in the name of Him who sent me, 'knowing not what may befall me and would not if I could.'"[33]

# Notes

## The Legend of Nancy Hart

1. The traditional description of Nancy Hart comes from both Elizabeth F. Ellet's *The Women of the American Revolution* (New York 1848) pp. 11, 227, 228, and George White's *Historical Collections of Georgia* (Atlanta 1854), pp. 441-444, 446. Both are cited in "Nancy Hart, Georgia Heroine of the Revolution: The Story of the Growth of a Tradition," *Georgia Review* VIII 8.4. (Fall, Winter 1954) Quotations of mentioned works will be those cited by Coulter.

2. A power of attorney given by Nancy Hart, recorded in the records of Clarke County, Ga., and witnessed by her son John and one other party, gives her name as "Anna Harte," with her "X" given by it (indicating she could not write). Given the varied spelling of the time, not to much should be made of the extra "e" but relevant is that in a legal document she used the name Anna, which was perhaps used interchangeably with Ann.

3. John Buchanan, *The Road to Guildford Courthouse* (New York, John Wiley and Son, Inc., 1997) p.86.

## Ol' Dan Tucker Was A Fine Ol' Man – And He Did Exist

1. Daniel Decatur Emmett biographical material provided by the Knox County Historical Society, Knox County, Ohio.

2. Colonial and genealogical records of the state of Virginia.

3. The George Tucker who moved to north Georgia and fought with Clarke is identifiable from Virginia records as the son of the Rev. Daniel Tucker's uncle William. The colonial records of North Carolina show the Tuckers in Wake County by at least 1765 and possibly earlier.

4. Deed Book 6, page 465, Mecklenburg County, Virginia, records the sale of May 9, 1785. Records of Wake County, North Carolina, has the elder Daniel Tucker dying in 1792.

5. "Ol' Dan Tucker," pages 157-161, *Georgia Scribe: Selected Columns of Herbert Wilcox,* Cherokee Publishing Company, Atlanta, Georgia 1974.

6. This and all subsequent material, direct or indirect, from Ron Pen was from an interview via email.

7. Howard L. Sacks and Judith Rose Sacks, *Way up North in Dixie: A Black Family's Claim To The Confederate Anthem* (Smithsonian Institution Press, Washington, D.C.)

## The Tragedy of Beverly Allen

1. Lloyd Dewitt Bockstruck, "Revolutionary War Land Grants Awarded by State Governments" (Baltimore: Genealogical Publishing Company, 1996) In his memoirs, the Rev. Peter Cartwright recounts staying at an inn in Hopkinsville, Kentucky, at which the innkeeper's wife was a sister of Beverly Allen.

2. Duane V. Maxey, "Beverly Allen: (The Sad and Sobering Story of an Early Methodist Apostate)" Digital Edition by Holiness Data Ministry

3. Ibid.

4. Ibid.

5. Ibid.

6. Robert Davis, *The Wilkes County Papers 1773-1833* The Southern Historical Press, 1979. P. 38.

7. Charleston (S.C.) *Evening Gazette*, 16 Feb 1786

8. Allen to Asbury correspondence, April 1786, Correspondence of Francis Asbury

9. Ibid, October 1786

10. Quoted in Maxey, "Beverly Allen: (The Sad and Sobering Journey of an Early Methodist Apostate" Biography of Robert Forsyth from website of U.S. Marshals Service.

11. Maxey

12. John H. McIntosh, *The Official History of Elbert County, 1773 – 1935* (Stephen Heard DAR Chapter Elberton, Georgia) pp. 71-72.

13. Memoirs of Peter Cartwright, quoted by Maxey

14. Ibid

15. Ibid

## Death Comes to the "Meanest Man in Georgia"

1. Taken from Mattox family history

2. The *Elberton Star*, Jan. 15, 1889 edition. John Harmer, editor of the Aiken (SC) *Standard*, wrote a letter to the Elberton paper giving his impressions of Elberton gathered on a recent visit to the city. He describes a meeting with William Mattox and describes him as "one of the finest educated men around …".

3. Mattox family records. Henry Mattox signed a note for the purchase of the property with Simeon Oliver on June 14, 1842, Elbert County deed book.

4. McIntosh's letter to Young Harris is cited on pages 113-114 of John McIntosh's The *Official History of Elbert County, 1790-1935*, copyright 1940, Stephen Heard Chapter of the Daughters of the American Revolution.

5. The account of Mildred Gray's loan to William Mattox and the Allen brothers' adventures in the North Georgia gold fields were related to Raymond E. Chandler, Jr., father of the author, in the 1930s by Overton Henry, an indirect heir stemming from Mildred Gray, who had passed some property to a nephew, Beverly Allen Henry, upon her death in 1887.

6. Details compiled by historians and archeologists employed by the U.S. Army Corps of Engineers prior to the building of Lake Richard B. Russell, which now covers much of the old Mattox property.

7. The account of the treatment of convicts at the Mattox stockade was related to a young Raymond E. Chandler, Jr., father of the author, in the 1930s by "Bud" Hilley.

8. McIntosh, pages 105-106.

9. The *Elberton Star*, July 23, 1889.

10. Description of Mattox from his biography in the official record of the 1877 Georgia constitutional convention, Georgia state archives.

11. The *Elberton Star*, July 23, 1889 edition

12. Mattox family records and *The Elberton Star*, June 8, 1889.

13. Economic profile of the 1890s from "The Depression of 1893" by David O. Whitten, Auburn University. Posted online by the Institute of Economics. The details of Mattox's financial fall family records.

14. Account of the gunfight drawn from the Nov. 22, 1900 edition of The *Elberton Star*.

## Murder in Milledgeville: The Rage of Marion Stembridge

1. The plans for the sesquicentennial and the description of Milledgeville on the morning of May 2 are drawn from the April 30 edition of the Milledgeville *Union-Recorder* and the May 1-3, 1993 weekend edition of the same paper.

2. *The Union-Recorder*, May 1-3 edition, 1993, "Murder-suicide shocked Milledgeville in 1953". The description of Stembridge's appearance, habits, and eyes are from author's interview with Eugene Ellis.

3. Drawn from synopsis of notes of Patti Wright, Georgia College & State University student who interviewed several of the surviving principals in the Stembridge case some years ago. The characterization of Stembridge is drawn from her interview of Judge Robert Green. The notes are found in the GC&SU archives.

4. *The Union-Recorder*, May 1-3, 1993, "Murder-suicide shocked Milledgeville in 1953".

5. *Macon Telegraph*, May 13, 1991, "'Paris Trout is about Milledgeville murders".

6. Narrative drawn from author's interview of Eugene Ellis, hereafter denoted as "Ellis".

7. From author's interview of Dr. Bob Wilson.

8. From author's interview of James Jossey.

9. *Macon Telegraph*, May 13, 1991, "'Paris Trout is about Milledgeville murders".

10. Summary drawn from notes of Patti Wright, GC&SU archives. Quote of Stembridge's sister-in-law is from *The Union-Recorder*, May 1-3 edition, 1993, "Murder-suicide shocked Milledgeville in 1953".

11. Notes of Patti Wright, GC&SU archives. Characterization of Stembridge is from transcript of Judge Robert Green interview.

12. Ibid

13. Ibid

14. Ibid

15. Ibid

16. Ellis interview.

17. Details of loan are from transcript of Wright interview of Eva Sloan. Quote from Ellis interview.

18. Narrative from Ellis interview.

19. Wright notes, GC&SU archives.

20. Drawn from Wright notes, GC&SU archives; divorce papers filed by both Sarah and Marion Stembridge, April 1953, and transcript of Green interview, GC&SU archives.

21. From transcript of Eva Sloan interview, GC&SU archives.

22. *The Union-Recorder*, Oct. 8, 1953.

23. Wright notes, GC&SU archives.

24. Wright notes and transcript of Eva Sloan interview, GC&SU archives.

25. Wright notes, transcript of Robert Green interview, both in GC&SU archives, and *The Union-Recorder*, May 7, 1953.

26. Wright notes, GC&SU archives.

27. Wright notes, GC&SU archives, and interview with Ellis.

28. Wright notes, GC&SU archives.

29. Wright notes, and transcript of Eva Sloan interview, both in GC&SU archives.

30. Transcript of Robert Green interview, GC&SU archives.

31. Wright notes, GC&SU archives.

32. Transcript of Green interview, GC&SU archives.

33. Interview with Ellis.

34. *The Union-Recorder*, May 1-3 edition, 1993, "Murder-suicide shocked Milledgeville in 1953", transcript of Eva Sloan interview, GC&SU archives, and interview with Ellis.

35. Wright notes, GC&SU archives; Ellis interview; Interview with John W. Grant.

36. Transcript of Robert Green interview, GC&SU archives.

37. Copy of Marion Stembridge's will and Wright notes, both in GC&SU archives, and interview with Ellis.

38. Jere Moore quote from *The Union-Recorder*, May 7, 1953.

# From A Georgia Chain Gang to The Great Escape

1. George Harsh, *Lonesome Road* (W. W. Norton and Company, Inc., New York), p. 192.

2. Pete Ehrmann, "The Thrill Killer," *Milwaukee Magazine* (December 2011).

3. Ibid

4. The *Atlanta Journal* (Jan. 20, 1929) "Harsh Sentenced to Die."

5. Laurel-Ann Dooley, *Wicked Atlanta: The Sordid Side of Peach City History* (The History Press, Charleston, S.C., 2014) p.76 and Harsh, p. 25.

6. Harsh, p. 25.

7. Ibid, p. 26.

8. Dooley, p. 77, and Harsh, pp. 26-27.

9. Dooley, p. 78.

10. Harsh, p. 27.

11. Dooley, p. 78, and Harsh, pp. 27-28.

12. Harsh, p. 28, and The *Atlanta Journal*, (Oct. 31, 1928).

13. Ehrmann, and Harsh, p. 29.

14. Erhmann.

15. David Beasley, "Mercy for Some" (excerpted from Without Mercy by the same author), *Atlanta Magazine* (February 2014) and The *Atlanta Journal* (April 1, 1929).

16. Harsh, p. 30.

17. Harsh, p. 9, and The *Atlanta Journal* (April 1, 1929).

18. Harsh, p. 18.

19. Ibid, pp. 52-57.

20. Ibid, pp. 20, 23-26.

21. Ibid, pp. 16, 18-20.

22. Ibid, p. 90.

23. Ehrmann, and Harsh, pp. 100, 111-115.

24. Harsh, pp. 120-123.

25. Ibid, pp. 129, 133.

26. Ibid, 154-159, 165.

27. Paul Brickhill, *The Great Escape* (W. W. Norton and Company, Inc., 1950) p. 34.

28. Harsh, p. 176.

29. Brickhill, p. 15.

30. Harsh, pp. 191-192.

31. Harsh, pp. 203-204, and Brickhill, p. 58.

32. Harsh, p. 203, 211.

33. Ibid, pp. 211-222.

34. Brickhill, p. 32, and Ehrmann.

35. Harsh, p. 201.

# Up From Slave Row – The Making Of William Henry Heard

1. Paul A. Cimbala, *Under the Guardianship of the Nation: The Freedman's Bureau and the Reconstruction of Georgia, 1865-1870* (University of Georgia Press, 1997), p. 45. In 1867, White would also found the Augusta Theological Institute, which would eventually relocate to Atlanta as the Atlanta Baptist Seminary and become the genesis of Morehouse College.

2. William Henry Heard, *From Slavery to the Bishopric in the A.M.E. Church* (privately published by the AME Church, 1924), p.89.

3. Ibid, pp. 19-20

4. Ibid, pp. 22-23

5. Ibid, p. 24

6. Ibid, pp. 28-29, Heard identifies Trenchard as "an Iowa man". This is another case where his recollection may be faulty, but with no real impact. The 1860 Census lists the then 37-year-old Trenchard as born in Georgia.

7. How long George Heard operated his shop near Elberton isn't clear. The 1870 Census data for Elbert County lists him as 57 years old, a mulatto, employed as a wheelwright, with an estimated net worth of $50. According to his son, he continued being a blacksmith, wheelwright and carpenter until his death, which Heard's memoir provides clues may have been about 30 years after the war.

8. Clarence L. Mohr, *On The Threshold of Freedom: Masters and Slaves in Civil War Georgia* (University of Georgia Press, 1986), pp. 253-254.

9. Heard, pp.31-32.

10. Ibid, p. 32.

11. Ibid, pp. 33-24.

12. Ibid, pp. 35-36.

13. *New Georgia Encyclopedia*, online: "Henry McNeal Turner".

14. Falechiondro Karcheik Sims-Alvarado, "The African-American Emigration Movement in Georgia During Reconstruction," Ph.D thesis, Georgia State University Department of History, 2011, pp. 3-4.

15. Heard, p. 90.

16. Ibid, p. 90.

17. Ibid, p. 39.

18. Ray Chandler, *The Last Days of the Confederacy in Northeast Georgia* (History Press, 2014), pp. 22, 105.

19. Cimbala, pp. 142, 320.

20. John McIntosh, *The Official History of Elbert County, 1790-1935* (Published by the Stephen Heard Chapter of the Daughters of the American Revolution, 1940), p. 124.

21. Heard, p. 40.

22. Ibid, pp. 36-37.

23. Ibid, pp. 41-43.

24. Ibid, pp. 38, 44.

25. Ibid, pp. 64-65.

26. Ibid, pp. 67-69. Heard's marriage was his second one, as he noted in his memoir. Oddly enough, however, he makes no mention at all in his writings of his first wife. The 1880 Census data for Athens, however, shows William Henry Heard married to Amanda Heard, and with a son, Wyatt Robinson. Whether the son was his own or a stepson, or why he doesn't mention either in his memoir, remains a mystery.

27. Ibid, pp. 71-77.

28. The *New York Times*, July 30, 1887, "No 'Jim Crow' cars".

29. Henry McNeal Turner, *African Letters* (Privately published by the AME Church, 1893) Turner letter of December 9, 1891, p. 73.

30. Heard, p. 49.

31. Ibid, p. 55.

32. Heard, p. 78, pp. 83-84.

33. Ibid, p. 88.